William C. Bouck
NEW YORK'S
FARMER GOVERNOR

William C. Bouck at 58, photographed by Matthew Brady in 1844. Bouck was an early subject of Brady, who went on to become famous as a Civil War photographer. Brady-Handy Photograph Collection, Library of Congress Prints and Photographs Division.

William C. Bouck

NEW YORK'S
FARMER GOVERNOR

Edward A. Hagan and Mark Sullivan
Edited by Lester Hendrix

HERITAGE BOOKS
2006

HERITAGE BOOKS

AN IMPRINT OF HERITAGE BOOKS, INC.

Books, CDs, and more—Worldwide

For our listing of thousands of titles see our website
at
www.HeritageBooks.com

Published 2006 by
HERITAGE BOOKS, INC.
Publishing Division
65 East Main Street
Westminster, Maryland 21157-5026

International Standard Book Number: **0-7884-3836-0**

Contents

Illustrations

Foreword

I prefer to call this a history rather than a biography. After all my research, I really do not know the intimate, the private William C. Bouck—what he thought, what his ambitions were, how he regarded his wife and eleven children. I have found little written by friends, associates or family. If he kept a diary, its whereabouts is unknown at this time. What we have is a fairly complete record of his accomplishments.

Edward A. Hagan
Middleburgh, N.Y.

Preface

This biography of Governor William Bouck, arguably the most important man from Schoharie county, has been years in the making. Edward A. Hagan worked on his history of Governor Bouck for more than twenty years, meticulously documenting and recording his findings with a persistency that rivaled that of Canal Commissioner Bouck. He left five thick binders of research materials and notes when he died in May of 2002, but only a brief text, for public speeches. The book needed completion and we selected Mark Sullivan to complete the text. Mark brought in his wife, Jamie, and Esperance town historian Kenneth Jones for assistance.

Governor Bouck rose from a rural upbringing and farming to become canal commissioner and governor of the Empire State. Then, he retired as an elder statesman. His dedicated and persistent effort to complete the Erie Canal places him atop the ranks of prominent Schoharie county residents.

We feel that this book does honor to Edward A. Hagan's work of twenty years and is also a long overdue honor to Governor William Bouck.

Stasia Hagan, publisher
Lester Hendrix, general editor

Middleburgh, N.Y.
May 1, 2005

Prologue

William C. Bouck saw drastic change during his lifetime. The world that he left in 1859 was vastly more complicated than that which existed on January 7, 1786, when he was born.

Born on a farm in the Schoharie Valley, he came from humble beginnings. And yet, through all the changes around him, Governor Bouck remained the same: a servant to the public and the people he represented in Schoharie county and the state of New York.

He is the only farmer to become governor of New York. He was also one of the most economical and watchful governors the people have been fortune enough to elect. These qualities come from his rural upbringing. His manner was plain and unpretending, yet dignified and graceful, and it won the confidence of everyone he met. One of the chief characteristics of the man was his fear of setting a bad example, or encouraging wastefulness, extravagance, or dishonesty.

Perhaps his attitude is best reflected by an article that appeared in the New York *Daily News*. Bouck described his experiences early in his first year as governor:

> *When I first entered upon the office, I was so engaged in trying to reconcile conflicting opinions, produce harmony in the party, and please everyone, that I paid no attention to my household expenses. At the end of the first three months, my quarter's salary was paid and my bills due were presented. To my utter dismay, the later exceeded the former.*
>
> *During my entire life I had made it a point never to spend more in a quarter than I received from my earnings. I believe that to be a good rule, and that, as Governor of New York, I should not transgress it and set a bad example, which might be the means of ruining thousands. I began to cast about, to see where I could cut down my expenses.*
>
> *The State officers had hired the house I occupied without consulting me, and the State paid the rent. I had nothing to say or do in that particular. The State officers who, because I was a country farmer, took particular pains to instruct me, told me I must bring my best span of horses and carriage from my farm in Schoharie, and ride in it, or I would degrade the high office to which the people had elected me. They also said I must have a*

colored waiter to attend the door of my residence, and a head cook and three or four assistants in the kitchen, and two or three chambermaids, besides a coachman to drive my carriage.

I remembered that during the entire quarter I had not found time to ride in the carriage with my family, except to church on Sundays, and then the coachman could not go to church, having to take care of the team. This I did not believe was doing exactly right, or setting a good example. I thought that myself and family could walk to church, as the distance was not great. We thereby would appear not to feel above others who walked, and, as the Governor's family, would be setting a better example than by riding. My wife also proposed to dismiss the chief cook and all the assistants but one, and she would superintend the cooking as she always had done on the farm; and my daughters proposed to dismiss the chambermaids, and they would do the chamber work. No sooner was this agreed on than accomplished.

The large bays and carriage went back to the farm in Schoharie, and the extra help were all dismissed. Everything worked like a charm. The colored door-man whom I retained assisted in waiting on the table. The State officers and my city friends did not observe but that all was as first arranged when they called. We walked to church, and greeted kindly all we met there, and enjoyed the services without thinking that the coachman could not attend them. We reduced our expenses to within my salary. I felt better immediately. I feel better now. I can discharge my duties better; and when my term of office expires and I return to private life, I shall feel that when I was governor of the State I did not set an example of extravagance in any respect which might be the means of ruining any one.[1]

Throughout the long period that he passed in public life, Governor Bouck set the example for prudence and discretion, honesty of purpose, practical ability, and unsullied integrity. These traits are, indeed, what helped him earn the esteem and approbation of his fellow citizens.

---

1. New York *Daily News*, April, 1859.

1. Youth

*Until I was twenty-two years of age, no common laborer on
my father's farm did more work than myself, either in clearing
land, or in the harvest field. Often have I gone to the plough before daylight, and from it after dark.[2]*

That is how William Bouck remembered growing up on his father's farm on Bouck's Island, Middleburgh, New York. Long days,
hard work, and perseverance were the only way to get anything accomplished. Throughout his life, he exhibited the ideals of sturdy
independence, patriotism, industry and perseverance that he inherited from his German ancestors. The future governor had acquired
the habit of hard work long before entering public service, an attrib-
ute that was to be a distinguishing characteristic of the man in later
years.

William C. Bouck was born on the seventh day of January, 1786,
on the family farm that had been occupied by his father and grandfather. Farm life was, for the most part, self-sufficient. The wood lot
furnished fuel and logs for the home. Homegrown flax, wool from
sheep, the spinning wheel and the loom made one's clothes. Residents grew vegetables and fruit, and hunted and fished. Religious
needs were taken care of by the circuit rider and news was spread by
word of mouth.

As farms clustered, hamlets formed. A community church was
built, then a parsonage, a schoolhouse, a tavern. Pathways became
roads that were almost impassable in the spring mud, and hamlets
grew into villages and became the center of economic life.

Bouck was the great-grandson of Christian Bouck, a German Lutheran who "fled from the rage of persecution in Germany."[3] He

---

2. John S. Jenkins, *Lives of the Governors of the State of New
York*. Auburn, N.Y: Derby & Miller, 1851, 693-694.

3. J. R. Simms, *Frontiersmen of New York*. Albany, N.Y.: George
C. Riggs, 1882, 38.

arrived in the county in the early 1700s. Christian's son and the future governor's grandfather, Wilhelmus Bouck, was the first male child born of white parents in the valley.

"Now being safely arrived in the first week, three children were born, namely Johanes Earhart, Wilhelmus Bouck and Elizabeth Lawyer, they found the land good, and much of the flats clear," wrote Judge John M. Brown in his 1823 *Brief Sketch of the First Settlement of the County of Schoharie by the Germans.*

The Boucks settled in Weisersdorf, the present-day Middleburgh. In 1755, Wilhelmus Bouck, Jacob Lawyer and Nicholas York patented from King George II about three thousand acres of land on both sides of the Schoharie Creek, now in the towns of Fulton and Middleburgh. Wilhelmus Bouck's share in this tract was inherited by his three sons, Christian (father of the future governor), John and William, and formed a part of the farm that would be owned and occupied by William C. Bouck.

Wilhelmus, the valley's first-born white male, lived through the revolution and had several close encounters with the British and Indians. One of the Indian raids in the Schoharie Valley was described by Josiah Priest[4] and published in 1840. This was just one of many such raids made during the revolution to destroy crops, haul captives back to Niagara, and bring fear to the doorsteps of the American supporters.[5]

---

4. Josiah Priest wrote a series of short pamphlets on the history of the revolution, including "The Captivity and Suffering of Freegift Patchin," "The Fort Stanwix Captive," "The Stories of the Revolution," and "A True Narrative of the Captivity of David Odgen." A first edition copy of a Priest pamphlet is extremely rare and valuable.

5. The historical accuracy of this is questionable. Most historians place the capture of W. Bouck in 1780. Roscoe states that Bouck was a widower by this time. But this could be a new raid never before mentioned in the histories. Either way, it is interesting.

The Story of Wilhelmus Bouck[6]

*About five miles below the bridge which crosses the Scho-
harie River in North Blenheim, N. Y., on a large and beautiful
island in that river, lived, in the time of the Revolution, Wilhelmus Bouck.[7] At this period Bouck and his wife were old people, who had in earlier times settled there even before the
French War. Now as this old couple lived there alone, it was not
a difficult enterprise for the mean and cruel Tories, with the Indians, their superiors, to capture this man and his wife as well
as to plunder his house. Accordingly, although Bouck lived on
an island, which was somewhat out of the track of the enemy,
and was as harmless as his age was imbecile, yet, they could not
pass him by, as the goods, as well as the persons were desirable
objects, with those ravening monsters, went and took them
away, goods and all to the wilderness. Their course was up the
river till they came near where the bridge above spoken of
crosses that stream, when they turned off toward the high lands
along the range of what is now called 'Westbrook', which heads
near the Jefferson Academy.[8] Here, having found a convenient
place, they camped down for the night. But as they wished to
rest a little, and to wash out their guns, they stopped some time
before night, on the same day of the capture. It was soon known
that poor Bouck and his wife had been carried off, which, when*

---

6. Josiah Priest, *Traits of the Revolution, With Stories of Hunters
in the New Countries and other Curious Matters of Truth.*
Langsingburgh, N.Y.: W.B. Harkness, Printers, 1840, 30-31.

7. Wilhelmus Bouck lived two miles from the Upper Fort in what
is now the town of Fulton, Schoharie county. Grandfather to Gov.
William C Bouck, Wilhelemus died in 1799. His son, Christian
Bouck, served in the 15th Regiment, Albany County Militia. Timothy Murphy, the hero of this story, became a close friend and business partner of the Boucks after the revolution.

8. Jefferson Academy, Jefferson, New York operated from 1817
until May 1851. "While the school was in progress it was one of the
best, and for those early days well sustained in numbers of schol-
ars." (Roscoe)

it was told to Colonel Vrooman[9] and Timothy Murphy,[10] of war-
rior memory, they made out a large party from one of the forts
and otherwise to go in pursuit of the villain. It was not a hard
task to follow their trail, especially for Murphy who could track
an Indian, on his way, however careful he might be with his
footsteps. Now as the sun was nearly going down, they found
that they had overtaken them, but without the Indians suspecting
it, as they had pursued them in a manner as silent as if there
had been but one man. It was seen, from the place where they
had halted, which was on a hole among the hills, that they had
taken the locks from their guns as well as the barrels from the
stocks, in order to wash them out, and to get them in readiness
for further massacres and murder.

Vrooman saw that they were in his power, and yet as he
feared they would kill the prisoners the moment the alarm
should be given, did not know how to begin the onset to prevent
such a fate. Here, at this critical point, Murphy desired to be
heard on the occasion, as that he believed he could name a plan
which would prevent their killing the prisoners, and also place
the old man and his wife out of the range of their shots. This
was a matter of very great moment, as well as of difficulty for
the prisoners, they saw were in the very center of the gang,
while they ranged around them nearly in a circle. Vrooman re-
plied to Murphy, in whom the whole party had the utmost confi-
dence, that by all means he should be happy to listen to his
plan. Murphy then said that were a few shots thrown over them
they would immediately fly to the woods, as it was out of their
power to return fire, as their guns were taken to pieces and lay
on the ground; and for the same reasons, they would not dare to

---

9. Col. Peter Vrooman, commander of the 15th Regiment, Albany
County Militia, was a veteran of the French and Indian Wars and
wealthy land owner of the Schoharie Valley.

10. A legendary frontiersman and member of the elite rifle corps,
Morgan's Riflemen, Murphy served in Col. Vrooman's 15th Regiment. Much has been written of Murphy; some of the stories strain
credulity and some bear suspicious resemblance to the tales told of
other frontier folk heroes. But enough of Murphy's exploits are veri-
fied by valid reports to make it certain he was an exceptional man
and soldier.

kill the old people, if they even remembered they had them at all – so great would be their fright. When this should be done, it was his advice, that the instant they sprang off, that the men whose fires were reserved, should, as quick as possible, select his mark and fire, as by that time the prisoners would be out of danger.

Vrooman consented, when a few shots were sent beyond them, the Indians and Tories looked up in awful alarm, and in a twinkling sprang for the cover of the woods. But as they fled, the reserved fires felled five of them, one of whom, as they after-wards found, was a white man; the rest had fled. They now re-took all they had, the prisoners, the guns of the enemy and all, and immediately set out on their return home, which they ef-fected that same night, so that the time of old Bouck and his wife, was of short duration, although it was somewhat fearful. In order to assist the old lady, as preparatory to the long jour-ney of the Canada route, they had cut off her clothes quite up to her knees, to enable her to walk in the woods, which the ordi-nary length materially retarded. This act might fairly be consid-ered as premonitory, to the taking of her scalp, should she grow weary on the way, as between the tomahawk and good speed, there was no half-way ground; in such cases, as the life of many a child, feeble woman, or old man, who was taken by the Indi-ans in that war, could prove; thus ended the captivity of Wil-helmus Bouck and his wife, of old Schoharie.

Christian Bouck, Wilhelmus's son and father of the governor, married Margaret Borst on November 23, 1785. She was descended from a German family which was among the first settlers of the Schoharie area. Christian Bouck served during the Revolutionary War as a sergeant in Captain Jacob Hager's second company, 15th Regiment, Albany County Militia. The militia protected the Scho-harie Valley from incursions of the British and Indians.

Johannes Bouck, a relative of Christian, also served in Captain Hager's company, as a lieutenant. He was called out on duty many times, including "the occasion to take Gen. Burgoyne, and the whole company started on their march, and when they arrived at Albany, they received the news that Burgoyne was taken prisoner; and before they left Albany, they saw Burgoyne brought there as a prisoner."[11] This occurred in the fall of 1777. Johannes continued in the service until the year 1781.

Another John Bouck opposed the American cause during the revolution and "soon after the commencement of the war, the said John Bouck, Sr., left the county and went to Canada as was supposed."[12]

ॐ

---

11. Johannes Bouck pension.
12. Johannes Bouck pension.

This portrait of Governor William C. Bouck, provided by the Temporary State Commission on Restoration of the Capitol, hangs in the capitol's Hall of Governors.

2. Public Servant

William Bouck's preparation for public service began at a young age. He attended common school in the winter and worked on the farm in the summers. This school was the first English speaking rural school in the town. He then spent a short period reading law in the office of George Tiffany, a former New York State senator, in preparation for taking the bar exam. State law at the time required seven years of study before someone could take the exam to become a lawyer. Bouck did not complete the seven years but had a solid foundation in law.

William Bouck began his public service in the militia of the state. The militia was comprised of part-time soldiers, like the National Guard of today. They were called up in times of emergencies and were required to drill with their units several times each year. Bouck was first commissioned as a lieutenant in Lieutenant Colonel Storm A. Becker's regiment on the first of May, 1807. Bouck would advance through the ranks during his service, serving as adjutant in Becker's regiment (April 12, 1809), and quartermaster of the 28th Brigade of Infantry (May 8, 1815). He was promoted to lieutenant colonel of the 18th Regiment, 28th Brigade of Infantry on April 24, 1817, and then colonel of the 18th Regiment on May 30, 1818.[13]

In the spring of 1807, at 21 years of age, Bouck was chosen clerk of Middleburgh and for the two following years, he was elected its supervisor. Clerk and supervisor were important positions in local government. Almost all official town business would go through these offices, such as tax collections, election and voting matters, and court proceedings. Bouck became widely known through his duties for the town. In 1811, he was nominated by the Republican convention for sheriff, which was then filled by appointment of the governor and council, but he declined for some unknown reason. The next year, he was a delegate to the senatorial convention held at Onondaga, and took an active part in its proceedings. In the same year of 1812, he accepted the office of sheriff and was duly appointed by Governor Tompkins and the Republican council. The Federalists removed him from office when they took power in the Council of Appointments in 1813.

---

13. William C. Bouck papers, 1727-1866. Division of Rare and Manuscript Collections, Cornell University library, Ithaca, N.Y.

Bouck's political career got a boost from his father's most intimate friend, Timothy Murphy, the skilled rifleman of Schoharie whose Revolutionary War exploits are still preserved in history, tradition and legend. The friendship of Murphy for the father descended to the son and it is said that the latter owed his first election to the assembly to the influence and zeal of his father's friend. For many years, Murphy exerted a powerful influence in the political ranks of Schoharie county and was active in bringing his young friend and neighbor into public notice. Of his will, Murphy's son Peter said, "He dictated on his deathbed to his friend William C. Bouck." The will is dated June 15, 1818. Bouck was also one of the executors of the will. One of Timothy Murphy's granddaughters married Charles Bouck, a son of the governor.

Bouck had become a leading politician in Schoharie county. Immediately after his removal from the office of sheriff in the spring of 1813, he was elected a member of the New York State Assembly by the people of Schoharie county. He was elected "to represent us in the Assembly because his known principles are American, and not British, or in other words, he is a true Whig which, at this time, is as important as in the first war."[14] He was twice re-elected to the same position, in 1814 and 1815, and returned a fourth time in 1817. One of Bouck's strongest points as an elected official was helping his constituents and keeping them informed about events in Albany. Lyman Hawes wrote to Bouck in April 1814, thanking him for assistance:

> *Sir,*
>
> *I have just received your letter which was no small satisfaction to me. I return your sincere thanks for your services as representative of our county. I congratulate you on your nomination as representative for the next session and you have my best wishes for your election on which I think there will be no doubt.*[15]

---

14. *Albany Daily Argus,* Albany, N.Y., Apr. 9, 1813. At the time, America was at war again with the British, the War of 1812. The first war was the Revolutionary War.

15. Bouck papers.

At the April election in 1820, he was elected a New York State senator, representing the then middle district of the state, and he was returned the following year.

Even as Bouck's political career developed, taking him away from Schoharie, he continued to maintain contacts and business interests in Schoharie. In 1813, he was chosen as a member of the board of directors for a company "building a bridge across the Schoharie Creek, in the Town of Middleburgh. The directors will meet at the house of Michael Borst for the purpose of receiving proposals for building the said bridge. By order of the board of directors, W.C. Bouck, treasurer."[16] He was appointed postmaster of West Middleburgh in April of 1821 and was very active with the Agricultural Society of Schoharie County, serving as its president when the organization was first organized in October of 1841. The society was interested in "procuring additional members to the society and promoting its objects generally."[17]

Bouck was also involved in the religious affairs of his community. He was a life-long member of the Evangelical Lutheran Church at Middleburgh and served as a Trustee for the Hartwick Seminary from its beginning in 1815 until his death in 1859. The Seminary, located four miles southwest of Cooperstown, taught upper level college courses in English, math, science, several foreign languages and also offered studies in theology.

Very soon after he entered public life, Bouck met Martin Van Buren. Both were in the legislature at this time and Van Buren became Bouck's political friend, a friendship that continued at least until the end of Van Buren's presidential term. The friendship was based on a shared political philosophy. Both believed in the ideas of Thomas Jefferson: decentralization of government, glorification of the rustic life, and humanitarianism based on a belief in progress.

In the legislature, Bouck was not distinguished as a debater. It was said he was rarely seen on the floor. However, in the committee room and in the private consultations of members, his judgment and vision were highly prized and were often of great service to his constituents. His shrewdness and tact, his prudence, and his address in the management of men were invaluable to his party.

---

16. *Schoharie Republican,* Schoharie, N.Y., Sept. 30, 1813.

17. Minutes of the Executive Committee of the State Agricultural Society, Oct. 26, 1841.

By an act of the legislature passed in 1821, provision was made for the appointment of an additional canal commissioner, assisting with the construction of the Erie Canal. The character of William Bouck for sagacity and ability as a businessman now stood so high that he was recommended for the new office, although he did not apply for it. Bouck received the unanimous nomination of the Republican legislative caucus and was chosen to fill the office.

The Schoharie *Observer* announced Bouck's appointment with this editorial, April 4, 1821: "We learn from Albany, that William C. Bouck is appointed Canal Commissioner, with a salary of two thousand dollars for his summer's work; this is in addition to his pay as Senator, and agent for the Hartwick fund, makes a comfortable income of at least three thousand dollars a year. When such fat things are in the market, how happens it that they are all engrossed by one man in this county?"

The appointment may well have seemed like an exile to Bouck, leaving the stimulating atmosphere of Albany to assume a job for which he had little training. He also may have worried about the prospect of his being away from his home and farm. The position was an important one but it held out little hope of future political advancement. Whatever his thoughts, the ex-farmer from Schoharie county was on his way toward an experience never to be forgotten.

∞

The locks at Lockport were among the great engineering feats on the Erie Canal. William C. Bouck was canal commissioner in charge of the section. From *History of the Canal System of the State of New York*, Noble E. Whitford, at http://www.history.rochester.edu/canal/bib/whitford/1906.

3. Canal Commissioner

Governor De Witt Clinton is considered the father of the Erie Canal, having pushed for its construction for many years. He believed the canal would create "great manufacturing establishments; agriculture will establish granaries, and commerce its warehouses in all directions. Villages, towns and cities will line the banks of the canal and the shores of the Hudson from Erie to New York. The wilderness and solitary will become glad and the desert will rejoice and blossom as the rose!"[18] The development of the canal system did indeed lay the groundwork for the rapid economic growth of communities along the canal route and throughout the state.

Construction of the canal was managed by five commissioners, each responsible for a section of the canal. The commissioners were appointed by the Legislature, "for the consideration of all matters relating to inland navigation."[19] They were authorized to acquire lands, procure loans for construction, and employ engineers and surveyors. They were also responsible for procuring maps, plans and cost estimates for constructing the canals; and securing lands or funds from the federal government, other states, businesses and individuals, to facilitate construction.

Construction on the Erie Canal began at Rome on July 4th, 1817, and continued until October 1825. The canal was 363 miles in length and was 40 feet wide at the surface, 26 feet wide at the bottom and four feet deep. Its 77 locks were 90 feet in length and 15 feet in width, admitting the passage of vessels 80 feet in length, 12 feet in width, carrying from 75 to 100 tons of cargo. The cost of construction was $7,143,789.00.[20]

William Bouck was appointed by the legislature as canal commissioner of the western section of the canal on March 29, 1821. It was with unfeigned reluctance that he accepted the office. The posi-

---

18. DeWitt Clinton, *The Canal Policy of the State of New York.* Albany, N.Y.: Bosford, 1821, 10.

19. Noble E. Whitford, *History of the Canal System of the State of New York, Together With Brief Histories of the Canals of the United States and Canada.* Albany, N.Y.: Brandow Printing, 1906, 4.

20. Ronald Shaw, *Erie Water West.* Lexington, Ky.: University of Kentucky Press, 1966, 75.

tion was an honorable but arduous one—full of responsibility and burdened with cares, perplexities and embarrassments. The western section of the canal covered construction from Brockport to its termination at Lake Erie, including the passage at the Mountain Ridge at Lockport, the most difficult part of the entire line due to the elevation and solid rock of the ridge.

The commissioners divided the canal into sections of one mile each. These were publicly contracted for, and the person who made the lowest bid was awarded the contract. Canal workers were boarded and fed by the contractors and were paid as low as half a dollar a day. Fourteen-hour working days were unbelievably difficult as the route of the canal went through marshes, virgin timberland, almost impenetrable underbrush, and muck. Most of the work was accomplished through sheer muscle power: the muscles of men, mules, horses, and oxen.

Contracts for the western portion of the canal were granted by William Bouck on August 2, 1822. The first actual construction work began on Friday, August 9, 1823. That morning, the citizens of Buffalo had an impressive ceremony to launch construction, with the firing of cannon and the hoisting of Old Glory. The happy contractors and canal commissioners were provided with liquid refreshments and the "grand canal," western division, was considered suitably launched.

The hardest part of the canal construction was the section at Lockport. The constructors would have to cut though a section of mountain ridge for three miles, which meant cutting through solid rock twenty feet thick. It was the greatest obstacle along the whole 363 miles of the canal. Blasting through the rock created a particularly tough problem due to the poor quality of the blasting powder. The canal commissioners had tried to save money on the price of powder but Commissioner Bouck would not accept this. He immediately ordered five hundred dollars worth of the better quality. The other commissioners made a fuss over this but the new powder was worth the price. The job got done. Fragment by fragment, workers banged and blasted through the rock.

Cutting through the rock, a series of ten locks were constructed raising the canal some 65 feet in the air. The locks were built in pairs so that boats going in opposite directions could pass each and not be delayed for long periods of time. These locks became a marvel of engineering, rivaling the pyramids in Egypt or the Coliseum in Rome. "Here the great Erie Canal has defied nature, and used it like a toy; lock rises upon lock, and miles are cut in the solid stone," noted a traveler in the 1830's.[21]

William Bouck hired Nathan S. Roberts as the expert engineer for the project.[22] Today we would call Roberts a trouble-shooter. Roberts had been one of the first to survey lands in the western portion of New York looking for a canal route, and had been working the last two years on the western most section of the canal, designing the terminal at Buffalo. Robert's labor force, around three or four thousand men, labored around the clock on the project at Lockport. At first, they were housed in tents, but as the enormity of the project became obvious, many decided to build permanent houses. Bouck also built a small cabin here, spending much of his time overseeing the progress of the locks. The prosperous city of Lockport arose from this chaos.

It was not until the fall of 1825 that the barrier of the Mountain Ridge and the locks at Lockport were finally overcome. This was the last obstacle between the Hudson and Lake Erie. "It was a grand site to behold, watching boats travel through the locks, one boat gradually rising to an elevation of sixty-feet, while another is seen, at the same time, sinking to an equal depth towards the spacious basin below."[23]

Commissioner Bouck did not sit in an easy chair in his office and superintend the work of the great enterprise, but personally went on horseback or on foot along the canal to inspect the excavations and see whether the contractors were meeting the specifications of their

---

21. Ralph K. Andrist, *The Erie Canal.* New York: Harper & Row, 1964, 117.

22. Bouck worked with some of the leading engineers of the day during his term as canal commissioner. Benjamin Wright, called the father of American civil engineering by some, was one of the first engineers selected to work on the canal, starting in 1817. He toiled for over twenty years on the project. Canvass White was another of the first engineers selected for the canal, working under Wright starting in 1817. White is credited for discovering waterproof cement, vital for keeping water in the canal locks. He was granted a patent for the cement in February of 1820.

23. Richard Weston, *A Journey West of Utica in the Mid-1830's,* 1833.

contracts. He frequently carried large sums of money and it was said that during the season of active operations, he carried as much as $100,000. Payments were made in cash, not in vouchers or checks. On many of his visits, he rode an animal that became famous as "Old Whitey" and indeed his horseback rides took such a hold on the public that newspapers soon alluded to the future governor as the "Old White Horse." Bouck was remembered by many in the region:

> *Who, at the west, who had cognizance of those times and their local events, does not remember how faithful and indefatigable he was in the discharge of his duties? Or, almost imagine that they can see him now, as they saw him in those primitive canal times, traveling the forest on horseback and on foot, from the log shanties of one contractor to those of another; sleeping and eating where emergency made it necessary, in quarters no matter how rude or humble; or in his room at the old 'Cottage' in Lockport, coolly and good-naturedly resisting the fierce importunities of the dissatisfied contractor; yielding to exigencies here and there, when public interest demanded it or strenuous and unyielding when it did not; pressing on the difficult work upon the Mountain Ridge, amid great difficulties preserving to the end, until he had seen the barrier removed that prevented the flow of the waters of Lake Erie through their long artificial channel.[24]*

On September 29, 1825, Bouck announced to the president of the canal board that the last unfinished parts of the canal, the section at Lockport, would be in readiness to admit passage of boats on the 26th of October.

> *To the honorable Stephen Van Rensselaer, President of the Board of Canal Commissioners*
> *Sir,*
> *The unfinished parts of the Erie Canal will be completed, and in a condition to admit the passage of boats on Wednesday, the twenty-sixth day of October next. It would have been gratifying to have accomplished this result as early as the first of September, but embarrassments which I could not control, have de-*

---

24. Orsamus Turner, *Pioneer History of the Holland Purchase of Western New York.* Buffalo, N.Y.: Thomas Jewett Co., 1849.

layed it. On this grand event, so auspicious to the character and wealth of the citizens of the State of New York, permit me to congratulate you.

Wm. C. Bouck,
Canal Commissioner
Lockport, Sept. 29, 1825 [25]

The work at Mountain Ridge and Lockport were completed on the evening of October 24, the guard gates were raised, and the filling of that level commenced. On the 25th, the entire canal from Albany to Buffalo was navigable.

The opening of the canal was marked by a grand ceremony. The canal engineers, the canal commissioners, all the leading politicians of New York, and finally, the grand champion of the canal, Gov. De Witt Clinton, traveled by boat from New York to Buffalo and then back again to New York on the canal. The trip of the "Seneca Chief," as the canal boat was named was probably one of the most thoroughly celebrated events in New York State. All along the route were jubilant people, making it a continuous holiday parade; ringing of bells and cannons boomed in every town along the canal; and Clinton was the hero of the fortnight.

At Lockport, the celebration was especially rewarding for Bouck and his group of engineers and workers. In fact, the packet-boat *"William C. Bouck"* was selected to be the first boat to pass through the locks at Lockport and ascend to the Lake Erie level to meet the boats from Buffalo that carried Governor Clinton and his suite on the return trip to NYC. "The last barrier is passed. We now have risen to the level of Lake Erie and have before us navigation open to its waters!" declared John Birdsall, a passenger on the *William C. Bouck.*[26]

William Stone, renowned historian of the period, was invited to participate in the celebration and record his thoughts. He described the festivities at Lockport:[27]

---

25. Bouck papers.

26. Whitford, 54.

27. Col. Stone traveled on the canal again a few years later, remarking "This traveling by canal boats is but a tedious process. The charm of novelty is soon lost, and the sameness becomes overpoweringly wearisome."

On the spot where the waters were to meet when the last blow was struck, and where the utility of an immense chain of locks was for the first time to be tested, the Celebration was in all respects to do honor to the work itself, and the patriotic feelings of the people. It is here that nature had interposed her strongest barrier to the enterprise and the strength of man. But the massive granite of the "Mountain Ridge" was compelled to yield. The rocks have crumbled to pieces and been swept away, and the waters of Erie flow tranquilly in their place.

At sunrise, on the morning of the twenty-sixth, a salute was fired from the mountain adjoining the locks, and all along the place was crowded with the citizens of the surrounding country; many individuals, too, from distant parts of this state, and from other states, attended the celebration at this interesting place. At nine o'clock, A.M. a procession was formed, under the direction of General P. Whiting, assisted by Colonel S. Barton, and Major M.H. Tucker, which marched to the grand natural basin at the foot of the locks, where the President and Vice-President of the day, the Canal Commissioners and Engineers, the Visiting Committee, and several distinguished citizens from abroad, embarked on board the packet-boat William C. Bouck; at the same time two hundred ladies were received on board the boat Albany; the rest of the procession embarked in the several boats lying in the Basin. This Basin, connected with the stupendous succession of locks, and the chasm which has been cut through the mountain, is one of the most interesting places on the route, if not in the World, and presents one of the most striking evidences of human power and enterprise which has hitherto been witnessed. A double set of locks, whose workmanship will vie with the most splendid monuments of antiquity, rise majestically, one after the other, to the height of sixty-three feet: the surplus water is conducted around them, and furnishes some of the finest mill-seats imaginable. A marble tablet modestly tells the story of their origin; and, without that vanity, which, though frequently laudable, is often carried to excess, imputes their existence to our Republican institutions.[28]

---

28. Cadwallader D. Colden, *Memoir Prepared at the Request of Committee, etc.* New York, 1825, 288.

20

The celebration continued east along the canal, finally reaching New York City. There, Governor Clinton poured a keg of water from Lake Erie into the Atlantic Ocean, journalists calling the act the 'Marriage of Waters,' officially opening New York State's first throughway.

> *Tis done! 'tis done! The Mighty chain*
> *Which joins bright Erie to the Main,*
> *For ages shall perpetuate*
> *The glory of our native State.*
> — *From* "Ode for the Canal Celebration,"
> *Samuel Woodworth, 1825.*[29]

Besides superintending the construction of the western section of the Erie Canal, Bouck was also selected by his associates to take charge of the work on the Cayuga and Seneca Canal, the Crooked Lake, the Chemung, and the Chenango Canals[30]. All of these canals were constructed under his supervision. Bouck also became convinced the Erie Canal was not large enough to handle the business of the growing west and was one of the first to suggest enlarging the canal to allow more traffic. Bouck would oversee the enlargement project as well.

For nineteen years, Bouck continued in office as canal commissioner. During that long period, he faithfully expended and accounted for upwards of eight million dollars, and rendered extensive and important services to the state in the construction of her public works. By his industry and devotion to the public interests, he obtained the confidence of the people in an eminent degree and retained it to the last. He probably did more personal supervision of the canal construction than any one man did. In addition, he became better known to more people than almost any other man in the state.

---

29. Colden, *Memoir*, 280.

30. Bouck hired another promising young engineer to work on the Chenango Canal, John B. Jervis (1795-1885), a pioneer in the development of canals and railroads for the expanding United States. Jervis designed and supervised the construction of five of America's earliest railroads, was chief engineer of three major canal projects, designed the first locomotive to run in America, designed and built the forty-one mile Croton Aqueduct (New York City's water supply for fifty years, from 1842-1891), and also the Boston Aqueduct.

People in the rural areas found in this part-time farmer one of their own kind, not a stuffy bureaucrat simply performing assigned duties. For Bouck, he found a chance to be in the open country, talking to common folk, which must have appealed to his genial nature. He was what the job required: a diligent administrator with strong attributes of honesty, understanding of men, perseverance, and warm geniality.

Bouck also could share a sense of humor to get the work done. Engineer John Jervis recalled one time discussing with Bouck and another chief engineer the trouble in finding qualified men to work the canal, especially the lock tenders. "The chief engineer remarked with much emphasis, "Those lock tenders have got no brains." Bouck, sitting by and listening to our conversion, coolly inquired, "How much do you pay your lock tenders?" The chief replied twelve dollars a month to which Bouck retorted, "Well, do you expect much brains for twelve dollars per month?"[31]

Cargo and travelers moved up and down the Erie Canal on packet boats. The packet boats were generally 80 feet long and 14 feet wide, and drew from one to two feet of water. The passenger boats had cabins which occupied the entire deck except eight or ten feet reserved for the cook and four to six feet reserved for the pilot. The cabins were eight feet high and had single berths on each side, calculated to accommodate from thirty to eighty passengers. The main room was used for a dining room during the day and a dormitory at night.

Passenger boats were drawn by three horses placed one before the other and traveled day and night, with relays every eight or ten miles, and made four miles an hour or 85 miles in 24 hours. Cargo boats did not generally exceed 55 miles a day. Travel on the canal was frequently congested so there was some discomfort in the overcrowding in the dormitories at night. But travel was much better than the jolting, dust, and other hardships of stagecoaches traveling by land. The Erie Canal route became the popular route as the tide of travel moved strongly from the eastern to the western states. Hundreds and thousands of settlers to Ohio, Indiana, Illinois, Iowa, Michigan, Wisconsin and other central states found their way west over the Erie Canal. The opening of the canal marked the beginning of the epoch of emigration from east to west.

---

31. Bouck papers.

Many travelers recorded their journey on the canal. One such was Thomas S. Woodcock,[32] who traveled along the New York frontier in 1836:

Packet Boat, these boats are about 70 feet long, and with the exception of the Kitchen and bar, is occupied as a Cabin, the forward part being the ladies Cabin, is separated by a curtain, but at meal times this obstruction is removed, and the table is set the whole length of the boat, the table is supplied with every thing that is necessary and of the best quality with many of the luxuries of life, on finding we had so many passengers, I was at a loss to know how we should be accommodated with berths, as I saw no convenience for anything of the kind, but the Yankees ever awake to contrivances have managed to stow more in so small a space than I thought them capable of doing, the way they proceed is as follows –

The Settees that go the whole length of the Boat on each side unfold and form a cot bed. The space between this bed and the ceiling is so divided as to make room for two more, the upper berths are merely frames with sacking bottoms, one side of which has two projecting pins, which fit into sockets in the side of the boat, the other side has two cords attached one to each corner, these are suspended from hooks in the ceiling, the bedding is then placed upon them, the space between the berths being barely sufficient for a man to crawl in, and presenting the appearance of so many shelves, much apprehension is always entertained by passengers when first seeing them, lest the cords should break, such fears are however groundless, the berths are allotted according to the way bill the first on the list having his first choice and in changing boats the old passengers have the preference.

The first Night I tried an upper berth, but the air was so foul that I found myself sick when I awoke, afterwards I choose an under berth and found no ill effects from the air, these Boats have three Horses, go at quicker rate and have the preference in

---

32. Thomas Woodcock, born in Manchester England, came to New York about 1830 and worked as an engraver. He took the most popular tour in America, drawing views along the canal from New York to Niagara. In 1846, he came into a family inheritance and returned to England.

*going through the locks, carry no freight, are built extremely
light, and have quite Genteel Men for their Captains. The distance between Schenectady and Utica is 80 Miles the passage is
$3.50 which includes board, there are other Boats called Line
Boats that carry at a cheaper rate, being found for half of the
price mentioned, they are larger Boats carry freight have only
two horses, and consequently do not go as quickly, and more-
over have not so select a company, some Boats go as low as 1
cent per Mile the passengers finding themselves.*

*The Bridges on the Canal are very low, particularly the old
ones, indeed they are so low as to scarcely allow the baggage to
clear, and in some cases actually rubbing against it, every
Bridge makes us bend double if seated on anything, and in many
cases you have to lie on your back. the Man at the helm gives
the Word to the Passengers. "Bridge" "very low Bridge" "the
lowest in the Canal" as the case may be, some serious accidents
have happened for want of caution, a young English Woman
met with her death a short time since, she having fallen asleep
with her head upon a box had her head crushed to pieces.[33]*

Cargo hauled on the canal got to its destination quicker and
cheaper than the land routes used in the past. "Goods which cost one
hundred dollars a ton carriage by wagon from Albany to Buffalo,
freights for six dollars in a fourth of the time. Below decks we carry
cargo for the asheries, both pot and pearl; and fifty bales of cedar
shingles for the fast-building town of Rome. We have fresh fish in
barrels for delivery in Rochester, and such general merchandise as
turnips, cloth in bales, gin in pipes, mirrors, furniture, axes, saws
and mauls, and ten fine head of merino sheep. Every few miles we
are hailed by farmers, standing on their private docks and offering
us goods for transportation or wishing to bargain for what we have
aboard. Only the Grand Erie Canal brings to this desolate region the
blessings of commerce and civilization."[34]

Beginning with modest revenue of $5,436 in 1821, the tolls pro-
duced annually increasing sums, the total for 1825 being $566,112.

---

33. Thomas S. Woodcock, *Some Account of a Trip to the "Falls of
Niagara" Performed in the Month of May 1836.* New York, 1840.

34. Samuel Hopkins Adams, *Grandfather Stories.* New York:
Random House, 1947, 274.

By 1830, the one million dollar mark was passed and the total revenue at the end of 1837 aggregated over fifteen million dollars, thus more than repaying the original outlay.[35]

Commissioner Bouck spent many years on the other canals in the western section of New York, canals that "feed" into the Erie Canal. He worked on the Cayuga Canal, the Seneca Lake and Crooked Lake Canal, Chemung Canal and the Chenango Canal. The Chenango Canal, which extended from Binghamton to Utica, crossed the Cherry Valley Turnpike at McClure Settlement. This canal was about ninety-eight miles long and had about one hundred locks. The cost was about two million dollars.[36] The canal was not a commercial success but many communities along its route did prosper due to its construction, including McClure Settlement. Although Schoharie county has done little to perpetuate the name of Governor Bouck, this small community changed its name to Bouckville in honor of canal commissioner Bouck (See Appendix B).

The impact of the Erie Canal and the feeder canals on New York were huge and the Empire State and the United States can trace much of their early growth to the canals. "New York was not always first in commerce and industry," wrote the state engineer, Roy G. Finch, in 1925. "The turning point came with the completion of the original Erie Canal." Growth of communities along the canal was phenomenal . Between 1825 and 1835, Albany, Troy, Utica, Syracuse and Lockport doubled in population, Rochester nearly tripled and Buffalo almost quadrupled. "The opening also clinched New York [City]'s position as America's premier port."[37] The canal demonstrated the ability of a self-governed people to execute a great public work. It gave an impetus to immigration and made possible the rapid settlement of the Northwest Territory, reduced cost of transportation and travel, and eliminated the hardships of stagecoach travel. It opened up farming areas to the north and south of its route and new mechanical techniques were devised to solve the special problems of canal building.

---

35. State of New York. *The Erie Canal Centennial Celebration, 1926*. Albany, N.Y.: J.B. Lyon Company, printers, 1928, 25.

36. Fitzsimmons, 109.

37. F. Daniel Larkin, *New York State Canals A Short History*. Fleischmanns, N.Y.: Purple Mountain Press, 1998.

William Bouck's greatest achievement was his contribution to the construction of the Erie Canal. At the centennial celebrations of the state, dedicating the new capital building in Albany, Bouck was remembered "as a man who was not hampered by the canal boards and canal auditor, but, trusted by his people, and putting into his saddle bag the money necessary to pay for work performed, mounting his old white horse, riding from one end to the other of the canals, not only to pay the workmen, but also to see that their work was well and honestly done; and as a good and faithful servant, rendering a just and true account for every cent expended—that man should be long and well remembered by the people of his State."[38]

When the Whigs secured a majority in both branches of the legislature in the election of 1840, it was proposed to remove William Bouck. The Whigs set about using the power of patronage by putting their political friends in office. Political consideration decided the question and he was removed during the legislative session that year to make room for a Whig successor. In fact, all of the canal commissioners and some of the engineers lost their jobs, replaced by political appointments. Nathan Roberts found them to be "wanting in experience, governed by political motives and not calculated to raise the reputation of the engineer department or the character of the Erie Canal improvement. They are aristocratic and political in their measurements throughout."[39]

⃓

---

38 Allen C. Beach, *The Centennial Celebrations of the State of New York.* Albany, N.Y., 1879.

39. Roberts become good friends with Bouck during their time together working on the canal. Roberts called Bouck a "man of great attention to business, of great discretion, and command of temper, discreet, economy, and preserving as a commissioner." In 1842 when Bouck was elected Governor, Roberts reacted with, "The Locos have treed the old Federal coons. Good!"

The "Marriage of the Waters" ceremony on November 4, 1825, celebrated the opening of the Erie Canal. Gov. Dewitt Clinton poured water from Lake Ontario into the Atlantic Ocean. From a mural at Dewitt Clinton High School, New York, posted at http://www.history.rochester.edu/canal/bib/whitford/1906/j02-05.html. © 1905, C.Y. Turner.

Dated September 1843, this poster advertises packet service between Lockport and Albany. Passengers from Niagara Falls could take the "cars" (train) to Lockport. The packets offered ventilators and sleeping quarters. "They surpass any thing ever put on the Canal." Edward Hagan collection.

4. Candidate For Governor

The people of New York State widely regretted the removal of "the Old White Horse."[40] His dismissal made Bouck a victim of the political system and a martyr. Public sentiment was strongly in his favor and the sympathies of his party were so warmly aroused that he was regarded as the prominent candidate for the gubernatorial nomination long before the convention in the fall of 1840. When the convention met at Syracuse in September 1840, he was unanimously nominated as the Democratic candidate for governor. Daniel S. Dickinson of Broome County was selected candidate for lieutenant governor.

Great excitement prevailed during the campaign. Countless grave and humorous missives were published and sung against Bouck and the party that nominated him. The election of 1840 brought out much political genius and wit, the likes of which had not been seen for many years before or since. Bouck, the rural farmer from Schoharie, was called the "Dutch Governor," "Krout Eater," and "Cabbage Head." A humorous article appeared in the Albany *Microscope,* a Whig paper, called the "Sour Krout (sic) Message," which made fun of Bouck's strong German accent and his rural upbringing. The article created no little merriment in the election commentary of the day. (See Appendix B.)

Despite all the negative campaigning against Bouck, the election was very close. Bouck's pollsters thought they would achieve victory. His son reported the feelings in New York City:

> *The Bastard Whigs are perfectly crazy; they are insulting you and have got to be perfectly braggarts. You cannot converse with them five minutes before they are like mad dogs, and begin*

---

40. A favorite white horse of Mr. Bouck carried the statesman wherever he had occasion to go, whether among his congenial Dutch neighbors in Schoharie or on his supervisory tramps on the canal route. Both his personal and political friends were in the habit of boasting that so kind was his heart, so affable his manner, so uniform his habit of stopping to exchange a few words with every poor laborer he met (and always in Dutch with Dutchmen), that the said old horse always stopped for this purpose, as a matter of course, without any rein or words of command.

to insult you by calling you everything they can think of. But we Loco Focos[41] are such good-natured fellows that we can stand it all and yet beat them. Our folks here are almost certain of your election. I believe you will be elected from 5 to 10,000 majority.

Yrs, CW Bouck,
Oct 4, 1840 New York[42]

In Schoharie, many of Bouck's friends and neighbors turned out to vote, supporting their local hero. The Rev. Dr. George Lintner, pastor of the Lutheran church in Schoharie and an influential religious leader throughout New York, voted for the first time in this election. He praised Bouck as a "pious man in all his daily pursuits. I gave him my vote from a sake of Christian duty."[43]

In the November election, 440,000 votes were cast. Bouck's opponent, Governor William H. Seward, was seeking re-election and defeated Bouck by a little over 5,000 votes. Although defeated in the race for governor, Bouck received more votes in New York than did the Democratic candidate for President, Martin Van Buren. Despite his defeat, Bouck continued to be the prominent candidate for the next gubernatorial nomination. For the first time in his life, Bouck was known throughout the state. The campaign may be considered as the real beginning of his political career.

After the election, Bouck went home to his farm in Fultonham. He continued correspondence with his friends and political allies, giving advice when asked, and kept informed with affairs of the Democratic Party. He became involved with some local activities, such as the agricultural society, and also traveled around the state giving talks.

---

41. "Loco Focos" was a name given to members of a faction that split off from the Democratic Party in New York State. They were bitterly hostile to the privileged classes that had control of Tammany Hall in New York City. They opposed monopolies and stood for pure democracy.

42. Bouck papers.

43. Lintner family papers, *Journal of Rev. Dr. George Lintner*, Wednesday, November 4, 1840. New York State Library, Manuscripts and Special Collections, Albany, N.Y.

As the convention of 1842 approached, Bouck was busy working his supporters. He wrote to a friend in the summer:

> *I cannot but feel decidedly interested in the passing events not because I am anxious for the office or the nomination, of which my name stands connected, but you know when a man merits recommendations for office, he does not like to be defeated. I am aware of the opposition at Albany but have been flattered with the assurance that these men do not fairly represent public opinion. Under the circumstances, I should be grateful to have a strong delegation from your county. It would show a spirit of independence. The people are tired of central cliques.*
> *Yr friend,*
> *Wm C. Bouck Fulton, 25 Jul 1842* [44]

Bouck and Dickinson were unanimously nominated again at Syracuse on Oct. 7, 1842. At the time, there were two factions in the Democratic Party: the conservatives or "Hunkers"[45] who favored completing public works projects and commencing other projects that promised to be profitable, but who did not favor increasing debt to a large amount; and the radicals or "Barnburners"[46] who were opposed to the construction of any work that would not pay for itself, and to any increase in the state debt. The main cause of difference was the spending for construction on the Erie Canal and the financial policy of the state. Bouck was a Hunker.

The Democrats had been out of office for so long that they showed an inclination to ignore their differences in order to muster the full party strength and thus regain control of the state government. Bouck was nominated as a compromise candidate—someone both factions could support and hopefully control if he won election in the fall.

As Bouck campaigned across the state, he emphasized that he was not averse to some extension of the New York waterway through borrowing. He knew that many of his supporters came from

---

44. Bouck papers.

45. Hunker is a corruption of the German "hunkerer"—one who desires, a selfish person. Hunkers were said "to get all they can and keep all they can get."

46. "Barnburner" was likened to the farmer who burned his granary to destroy the rats.

the areas where canal construction was popular. But he still had to appease those who supported the official "stop and tax" platform of the party[47]—no additional canal construction in the State. Bouck tried to steer a middle course, paying lip service to the official party stand but also suggesting special cases and exceptions where construction might be good economy.

Bouck spent the fall traveling about the state, giving talks to county organizations and gathering support for his campaign. He worked with the local officials to get out the vote, as one supporter in Johnstown reported in October 1842:

Dear Sir,
> *There are several old revolution soldiers which must be brought in with teams. I have agreed to drive two wagons on Election Day. I must have three wagons to fetch some. I will vote early in the morning then fetch them down.*
> *Vincent Quackenbush, Johnstown.[48]*

The campaign generated much discussion in the papers leading up to the election. The *Albany Daily Argus*, a Democratic paper, endorsed Bouck and Dickinson and wrote favorably about them.

> *For us, Col. Bouck needs no commendation— no certificate of ability—for his history is known to all. It has been identified with the growth and prosperity of our forever safe and judicious system of internal improvements. To this, he has ever been a stable and efficient friend. For nineteen years, he held an important and responsible station on our public works, and during that time, discharged the duties of that office with an integrity so scrupulous—with a conduct so exemplary—with a foresight so statesmanlike, and with a skill so decided—that he enjoys the enviable reputation of being one of the most invaluable public servants ever employed in the service of the state.[49]*

---

47. The "Stop and Tax Law" of 1842 was a controversial statute that stopped all canal construction not deemed absolutely necessary, pledged a portion of canal revenues to pay the state debt and established a small property tax to rehabilitate the state general fund.

48. Bouck papers.

49. *Albany Daily Argus,* Sept. 12, 1842.

Another Albany paper, the *Evening Journal*, a Whig paper, supported Luther Bradish, the lieutenant governor under Gov. Stewart and Whig candidate. The paper ran a column nearly every day, entitled "Bouckania," which carried amusing tales of Bouck's upbringing. These anecdotes ridiculed Bouck and his "old white horse."

> *The admirable Bouck—we think the people of this state will be amused at these anecdotes which are published to show the democracy of costume, and the simplicity of character and habits of the regency candidate for governor.*
>
> *Now while we do not wish to detract an atom from any positive merits or well earned fame of Col. Bouck, we must be allowed to say that these anecdotes exhibit no very striking qualification for public favor.[50]*

Another "old horse" story appeared in the Albany *Evening Journal* on October 26, 1842:

> *A Wonderful Horse! This story relates to a quadruped in the possession of Mr. Bouck—On arriving at his residence, we found that he had gone over the mountain five or six miles on foot, and while waiting for his return, we amused ourselves with looking around his farm. "There," says my friend, "is the old white horse. I wouldn't drive that horse twenty miles along the Mohawk to have him. I should stop and talk half an hour with every laborer I met. The horse wouldn't move until I had done so."*
>
> *Who would have supposed that a brute beast could be so well trained to the business of electioneering!? If the story be true, we shall be disposed to think that the Regency missed a figure in not nominating the old white horse instead of Col. Bouck, as their candidate for Governor!*

The election results took several weeks to compile throughout the state. The early returns showed the Bouck and Dickinson ticket off to an early lead, as reported in the *Albany Daily Argus*:

> *Benighted Schoharie comes proudly into the ring. She manifests her attachment to her favorite farmer by a majority of*

---

50. *Albany Evening Journal*, Oct. 24, 1842.

1195 votes. His majority in 1840 was 832. So much for the "Old White Horse."[51]

Bouck won the election by nearly 22,000 votes over Luther Bradish. There were 401,426 votes cast for governor of which William Bouck received 208,072 and Luther Bradish 186,091. Gov Stewart received 7,263 write-in votes. Bouck's success was truly remarkable. He carried forty-three counties while Bradish won in only fifteen. This shift represented a gain of nineteen counties for Bouck over the 1840 election. It was something of an individual triumph for a man who previously had been only a party follower. His perseverance in defense of the party had been rewarded and his honest and diligent service given due recognition.

As soon as the election was over, Governor-elect Bouck was besieged by friends and political supporters looking for political appointments, especially his 'life-long friends.' One friend wrote:

Dear Sir,

It is with feelings of long cherished friendship arising from our old acquaintance with your Excellency while in our juvenile days, while we were school mates receiving our literary instruction from the same teacher and participating in the sports and festivities of boyhood and youth and which early friendships has by no means been abated by the lapse of years that I congratulate your Excellency upon your election.

My pecuniary circumstances are somewhat embarrassing. Consequently I have been induced, by the advice of my political friends, to become an applicant for the appointment of one of the turnkeys in the state prison at Auburn. While I would by no means ask or expect of your Excellency to interfere in so small concerns, yet I do humbly solicit any recommendation your Excellency might feel justified in giving of my moral and political character.

Yr friend,
Peter Zielie 13 Dec 1842[52]

Another friend, in dire straits, asked for a serious appointment:

---

51. *Albany Daily Argus,* Nov. 10, 1842.
52. Bouck papers.

*For the last three or four years past has been the most
gloomy, heart-rending and sorrowful of my whole life. Every little ray of light that filtered across my path upon which I fixed
my hopes of deliverance has almost in every case instantly van-
ished and has only served to sink me deeper and deeper in ruin.
I venture to make one more respectful request for an office, and
that is the office of Adjutant general. If you give me this office,
you will make me and my family happy and if you withhold it,
we must become wretched and miserable for I see no alterna-
tive, my property must be sold and I and my family turned into
the street and for aught I know will become city paupers.*
> *Respectfully your servt,*
> *Abraham Keyser, Albany 22 May 1843.[53]*

The *Schoharie Patriot* could not help but notice all this activity:

"Dec. 23. Col Bouck, governor elect, left this place on Saturday
last for Albany, preparatory to his entering upon his duties of office
on the first of January next. Applicants for office, it is said, are as
busy as bees in this county, getting their friends to endorse their
claims, etc. Fearing there would not be vacancies enough in the
State to supply all, some particular favorites we learn applied to
'Uncle William' to help them snug berths under the United States
government. Well, 'Uncle William' will try, no doubt."[54]

In the meantime, Governor Seward commenced preparation for
his leaving Albany. His private secretary was busily aiding him in
completing his correspondence, arranging his papers and turning
over the business of the state to Governor Bouck. On December 23,
1842, Seward wrote:

*Governor Bouck arrived here on Saturday; on Tuesday, he
called upon me. His manners are easy and fascinating, and I
think he lacks neither dignity nor grace; but my taste, you know
differs from the prevailing one. He is evidently a kind, honest,
amiable, and sagacious man. He was at first quiet, reserved,
and manifested a sense of restraint. I told him much that was
important to know, tendered to him every explanation and aid,
and assured him that, do as he might, I would never write at
him in the newspapers as my predecessor had written against*

---

53. Bouck papers.

54. *Schoharie Patriot*, Dec. 23, 1842.

me. The good man relaxed... His house is neatly furnished...
Mrs. Bouck came to town a day or two since. I call upon her
tomorrow. She has a daughter who was educated at the Critten-
den School here, and who will soon be a belle.[55]

The city of Albany was then a rapidly growing community of about 15,000 people. Built on a side of a steep hill which local boosters insisted upon calling a gentle elevation, it was the political heart of New York State. The capitol, at the head of State Street, was its very center. It was a solid, three-story building with an imposing facade. From the public square on which it stood, all the important centers of activity in the town could be observed.

When he arrived at Albany to assume his new duties, "Old White Horse" was fifty-eight years of age. He was of medium height, an extremely low forehead, small gray eyes, and a tremendous stock with shaggy iron-grey hair, which stood erect upon his head in all directions.[56]

Governor and Mrs. Bouck soon discovered how expensive it was to set up a household in the governor's mansion in Albany. They were provided a house at 119 Washington Street by the state but had to pay $300 a month for the "neat" furnishings.[57] Their expenses for the first week show:

Cash paid for wood		$94.00
Cash paid for 2 work woman		
for cleaning house		5.00
Cash paid for hay		6.25
"	upholstery	44.50
"	oil cloth	25.53
"	man sawing wood	3.00
"	for sofa in north parlor	55.00
"	for brushing carpets	3.00

---

55. Frederick Seward, *W.E. Seward an Autobiography 1801-1846.* New York: Derby & Miller, 1891, 642-643.

56. Beman Brockway, *Fifty Years in Journalism Embracing Recollections and Personal Experiences.* Watertown, N.Y.: Daily Times Printing, 1891, 53.

57. John A. Garraty, *Silas Wright.* New York: Columbia University Press, 1949, 328.

He paid for some other household furnishings and supplies, bringing his total for the week to $543.41.[58]

This came as a great surprise to the rural farmer from Schoharie county. Governor Bouck, as commander-in-chief of the state militia, also had to pay for his uniform and assorted equipment:

1 pair of gold Epaulettes 3 stars	$15.00
1 yellow swain fountain plum	9.50
1 gold staff sword	20.00
1 gold acorn sword knot	2.75
1 pair fine gold spurs	2.30
1 pair fine buff gunnels	5.00
1 epaulette box	1.50
1 Coat and vest	39.20
Total for commander-in-chief uniform[59]	$95.25

On January 1, 1843, he took the oath of office as governor with a ceremony at the state capitol. "The morning was intensely cold, marking 12 degrees below zero but towards noon the weather moderated, and though snow continued to fall during the whole afternoon, it did not interfere materially with the business of the day," reported the Albany *Evening Journal* on January 3. Governor Bouck, his friends, Lieutenant Governor Dickinson, the secretary of state, the chief justice, and others, along with Governor Seward, all stood at the head of the staircase in the great hall. "Gov. Bouck was administered the oath of office. As he laid down the book, Seward stepped forward and shaking him by the hand, congratulated him upon the high distinction conferred on him by the people, and expressed the hope that his administration would succeed and bring prosperity and happiness to the state. Gov. Bouck thanked him for his courtesy and good wishes, and exchanging bows, they separated. So unusual had any such proceedings hitherto been that the audience, taken aback, stood in open-mouthed surprise at the spectacle of such an exchange of courtesies between a Whig and a Democratic Governor."[60]

---

58. Bouck papers.

59. Bouck papers.

60. Seward, 642-643.

Governor Bouck and his party then went to the gubernatorial residence for a reception of citizens and well-wishers that continued throughout the day. A new musical number was unveiled in honor of the new governor, "Governor Bouck's Grand Quick Step," performed by the National Brass Band of Albany.

Governor Bouck got down to business the next day. His administration opened with the delivery of his annual message to the legislature. It was the custom of governors to draft their messages and then submit it to the state officers. This was always done at the residence of the governor or at the executive chamber. On these occasions, the messages were read over carefully and freely criticized; new suggestions were offered and corrections were often made. Governor Bouck did not depart from this practice. After finishing his message, he invited the state officers to his residence. They declined but required him to meet them at the state hall. He complied. The state officers, both Whig and Democratic alike, were testing the new governor to see who would be in charge of the state government. The message was read but no alterations or suggestions were made. The Bouck administration was off to a rough start.

The message itself had been dictated by ex-President Martin Van Buren, who wanted a united party. Bouck applied for guidance to Mr. Van Buren promptly after the election. Van Buren's reply, the original draft of which, dated December 7, 1842, is still preserved, much underlined and annotated,[61] gave Bouck rather more than a skeleton outline, with suggestions such as "Here insert figures of State debt," for the Governor's other advisers to supply. It was a rather colorless document, largely focusing on national topics and presenting few specific suggestions for reform or change in state affairs. His message was immediately criticized by both sides in the daily papers[62].

---

61. Martin Van Buren manuscripts, Library of Congress, Vol. XLIV, doc. 10434.

62. Gov. Bouck was not a favorite politician of the press. Beman Brockway, who spent fifty years covering the Albany political scene with the *Evening Journal,* describes Bouck as "a very ordinary man. He was well disposed, no doubt, but few persons, I venture to say, ever spent fifteen minutes in conversation with him who did not come to the conclusion that he was a mighty small pattern of a man for governor of the Empire State."

"Governor Bouck's message was very different from the productions of most of his predecessors. It was much shorter, made no pretension to literary style, and indulged in fewer 'Glittering generalities' on the philosophy of government, but was notably direct and lucid in expression and instinct with shrewd sense," the *Albany Evening Journal* commented.[63]

"Although shrewd, honest and sincerely and diligently devoted to the public service according to his light, he was somewhat narrow in his views, had little force of character, and was void of the essential capacity of leadership," the *Albany Daily Argus* said.[64]

Governor Bouck opened his message with an introduction of himself:

> *For the first time since the organization of the government, the Chief Magistrate has been selected from the agricultural portion of the community. Whatever distrust I may feel in taking upon myself an untried station of so much importance and difficulty, I repose with confidence on the guidance of the Almighty; on the co-operation of every department of the government, and on the indulgence of a generous people, who are always ready to overlook unintentional errors.[65]*

In the annual message, Bouck had recommendations on the subject of internal improvements by roads and canals to the legislature but cautioned against increasing the state debt unwisely.

> *I recommend to your careful and attentive consideration the subject of internal improvements by the roads and canals, which are eminently calculated to aid the enterprise and promote the welfare of the people. But in making this suggestion, I must not be understood as recommending extravagant expenditures, or ill-advised undertakings. The system should have for its object the general welfare. A public debt is under all circumstances objectionable, and should never be incurred except upon the most weighty considerations. The Legislature of 1842 convened at a period of great embarrassment in the financial affairs of*

---

63. Jan. 3, 1843.

64. Jan. 6, 1843.

65. Charles Z. Lincoln, ed. *Messages from the Governors.* Albany, N.Y.: J.B. Lyon, 1909, IV, 15.

the State. The treasury was empty; our credit seriously impaired; the State stocks were selling at ruinous sacrifices; temporary loans were nearly at maturity; the time for the quarterly payments of interest on the public debt, amounting to more than $20,000,000, was fast approaching; contractors were pressing for payment, and the progress of the public work virtually suspended. Under such circumstances to have continued large expenditures, or indeed any not demanded by imperious necessity, or good economy in reference to the condition of the public works, and that good faith due to our citizens with whom the state had existing engagements, would in my opinion have been a wanton disregard of public duty.[66]

Gov. Bouck went on to recommend several projects be funded and completed for the general good of the people. "I am convinced that completion of the unfinished work at the Schoharie Creek, at Sprakers, at Canajoharie, Fort Plain, the Indian Castle Creek, at Syracuse, the work connected with the reduction of the Jordan level, at Macedon, and at Lockport, would be essentially useful and some of it may be indispensably necessary. This should be done with strict reference to the financial condition of the State."[67]

Besides raising the question of construction policy, Bouck showed interest in other reform issues. First was the issue of militia reorganization. Bouck recommended measures for the encouragement of the voluntary organization of uniform companies to make them more efficient. "I am inclined to the opinion that if the militia laws were so amended as to keep up an organization, by a perfect enrollment, and a full corps of officers, and dispense with all the trainings, excepting an annual meeting by regiments for the propose of inspection and review, it would relieve the community from a burden, for which there appears to me to be no equivalent."[68]

Another reform issue concerned the public school system. Previously, schools had been administered by county commissioners and inspectors. The teachers were appointed by the commissioners, and they were required to have no formal educational training. The costs of public education were paid from rate assessments on each county

---

66. Lincoln, 15.

67. Lincoln, 16.

68. Lincoln, 21.

and revenue from the state funds. Bouck made no specific recommendations this year, leaving any changes up to legislative decision. As we shall see in his message the following year, he came up with some specific proposals that were carried into law.

He also issued a proclamation that Thursday, December 14, was to be observed as a day of prayer, proclaiming "a day of praise and thanksgiving to almighty God for the numerous and numerated blessings of the year. For the distinguished blessing we have enjoyed, we should raise our heart in humble adoration to our father in heaven; thereby presenting to the world the imposing spectacle of the entire state abstaining from all secular engagements and devoting themselves to the service of the Almighty."[69]

ဆ

---

69. *Schoharie Republican*, Nov. 21, 1843.

Bouck family homestead at Fultonham. The negative is dated 1865. Mark Sullivan collection.

5. Administration of Governor Bouck

In his message, Governor Bouck endeavored as judiciously as possible to avoid any conflict or dispute on any major issues of the day, while adhering to the platform laid down by the convention which nominated him. The result was that instead of healing the breach in the party, he made it worse. The breach between the governor and the political leaders of both factions, the Barnburners and the Hunkers, then became marked and decided, and neither side seemed desirous of consulting with or advising the other; both factions were now alienated from him. The unity that seemed to prevail in the campaign was entirely superficial. During the two years of Bouck's administration, the Democrats had control of both branches of the legislature, but the contest between the Barnburners and the Hunkers interfered with much of the legislative business.

Even though the Democrats had united to defeat the Whig Bradish, it soon became evident that a collision would take place between the two factions of the Democratic Party. Being the first Democratic executive after a Whig administration of four years, Bouck was called on to exercise the appointing power to a greater extent than his predecessors. He had to replace all the Whig political appointees who were removed from office because of the Democratic victory at the polls. It was impossible for him to avoid incurring the hostility of those who were disappointed. Governor Bouck had to make fifteen hundred appointments for which there were twelve thousand applicants, and the disappointed office seekers became part of the organized opposition.

Bouck was not a practical politician. Like many men in his situation, he seems to have been impressed with the idea that he could bring together and harmonize conflicting factions, and at the same time make the support of his administration the test of party fidelity. This was a great flaw.

The governor made a political mistake in trying to conciliate those of his own party opposing his administration. He also left the choice of appointments entirely to county committees, even when they were hostile to him, another mistake.

It was expected that Bouck, a Hunker, would find his official associates in the ranks of that faction. Immediately after his election, the Barnburner press began discussing, suggesting, and all but dictating who should be his appointees to office and who should be his advisors. The unity that seemed to prevail in the campaign of 1842 was entirely superficial and the resolution of the convention approving his administration was merely a campaign device.

The appointment with the most importance—and one carrying a substantial salary—was adjutant general. At the time this officer, besides governing the militia, was also the confidential executive assistant to the governor. There were many influential candidates for the post, and Bouck appointed Lyman Sanford of Middleburgh, who was married to Bouck's eldest daughter. It was a purely personal choice. In the eyes of the opposition, the marriage relationship was Sanford's one great liability. It was angrily demanded in the press how many more "Dutch Cousins" were coming to Albany. The Barnburners united with the Whigs to defeat the nominations of Governor Bouck to which they objected. The opposition was increased from then on, by voting down any law Bouck endorsed, irrespective of the merits of the case but wherever it might make the most trouble.

The *Schoharie Patriot* reported Governor Bouck's first appointments on January 6, 1842:

> *Governor Bouck has appointed Lyman Sanford Esq., his son-in-law, Adjutant General of the State; James M. Bouck is his Private Secretary; C.W. Bouck his Military Secretary; and his nephew had been appointed Messenger. Two sons, one son-in-law and a nephew snugly provided for. Who so provideth not for his own and especially his own household, is worse than an infidel.*

Gov. Bouck received word of the displeasure in letters from his friends:

"A general outcry against the governor and a sufficient quantity of steam has been let off. You have excited such displeasure and I am invariably rewarded as follows: 'do not like his message, do not like many of his appointments, do not like the manners in which others have managed him, do not like the great length of time taken up in making appointments, and will not vote for him again.'

"Yrs, J. Webster, March 5, 1843 New York"[70]

---

70. Bouck papers.

After the legislative session, Bouck traveled to the agricultural state fair in Rochester with Martin van Buren. They did not receive a warm welcome. Barnburners approached the Governor only to deride and insult him, and even Van Buren was neglected because he was with the 'Hunker' chief executive.

Governor Bouck opened his second year with an annual message free of any Van Buren interference. It was a very able state paper written in a superior style. Bouck had solicited input from all across the state, asking for suggestions and ideas from political friends and allies. He wrote letters to all the county commissioners and received dozens of letters in reply, telling of local problems that needed addressing as well as state and national concerns. He also received advice on the type of message to deliver this letter from the Erie county commissioner:

"Sir, I regard brevity and precision in the annual messages capital points. I am aware the great and diversified interests of the state will not permit of a short message. The desire of brevity and precession should not induce the executive to overlook any prominent interest nor lead him to withhold any well-reasoned suggestion or exchange or improvement.

"Jared Birdsall, Nov. 18, 1843, Buffalo"[71]

* * *

The second annual governor's message differed from the first in tone and content. There were fewer attempts to conciliate and more explicit recommendations. He advocated more concrete actions. The change was probably based on Bouck's having learned from experience that opposition could not be avoided.

The message's most striking feature was its recommendation concerning the canals. Bouck knew this would be a thorny issue with the legislature but he met it head on, laying down a concrete program of action. He had been associated for many years with the canals and was a believer in the system. He was committed to the policy of maintaining the canals and making the improvements that were needed in them as far as the surplus revenues of the state would permit. He recommended that the Schoharie aqueduct be completed, that the Black River and Genesee Valley canals be finished and most important of all, that the Erie Canal locks be

---

71. Bouck papers.

enlarged and other improvements made to meet the demands of constantly increasing commerce.

"Where new structures are so nearly finished, that it would cost less to complete them than to keep in repair the old ones they are designed to supercede, they should, in my judgment, be put in a condition to be used. Under this impression, I recommend that the Canal Board be authorized to complete such new works, as in their opinion can be done with better economy, than to sustain those designed to be superceded."[72]

The message also recommended several amendments to the state constitution. There was a strong movement afoot to hold a constitutional convention. Bouck did not regard this as necessary or desirable, but he suggested the adoption of amendments to the constitution. He recommended amendments to increase the efficiency of the judiciary of the state, saying "perhaps no feature of the Constitution is so likely to require revision and adaptation to the growth and advancement of the State, as that organizing the judicial system." Bouck recognized that the courts were being overburdened with cases and that "adequate provision should be made for the prompt and efficient administration of justice."[73] One recommendation to ease the burden was to add two associate chancellors with full power to the Court of Chancery. A second proposal was for two additional justices of the Supreme Court. "It is generally agreed that some amendments in relation to the judiciary are necessary, and I recommend the subject to your early and careful consideration," the governor said.[74]

Bouck had suggestions in other areas as well. He proposed a system of checking expenditures to prevent the incurrence of a state debt or the expenditure of public funds for other than the ordinary purposes of the state, except by vote of the people. He recommended the modification and alteration of the safety-fund law to secure better protection against losses from bank failures, and the improvement of the militia. In addition, he advised the passage of a law directing the locks on the canals to be closed on the Sabbath, provided it was thought by the legislature that such a law could be enforced.

---

72. Lincoln, 75.

73. Lincoln, 55.

74. Lincoln, 76.

One last area in which Bouck showed interest was care of the mentally ill. He always had a humanitarian interest in helping the unfortunate of the state and went to great trouble to secure the best facilities for handicapped citizens. Previously, he had been notified that only one-third of those in need of care in the state could be accommodated decently in existing institutions, and he proceeded to bring the matter to the attention of the legislature. He suggested construction of additional facilities and further stated that every institution should have a promenade ground.[75]

Despite all the political bitterness of the first year, Governor Bouck was able to push through beneficial legislation. In response to his proposals, the legislature approved a constitutional amendment providing three officers for the Court of Chancery, approved the two additional justices to the Supreme Court, and approved limiting state debt to a million dollars unless approved by a special vote of the people, excepting debt incurred for suppressing insurrection or repelling invasion. A new facility for mentally ill at Flatbush, Kings county, was started, along with two additional buildings at the state's Utica facility.

Bouck also led the fight to make changes in the state school system, one of the most important social reforms of the decade. During his administration, common schools were expanding rapidly, and there was increasing dissatisfaction with the quality of teachers. Bouck proposed streamlining and abolishing the offices of school inspector and school commissioners. In their place, the office of town school superintendent was created. The new system offered better means of inspection on the local level. It also provided for new school buildings and standard texts across the state. The legislature also passed a bill providing a 'normal school' at Albany, a small school of 200 to 400 students creating an institution whose object "was the instruction and practice of teachers for common schools in the science of education and in the art of teaching." It was the forerunner of the University at Albany and the State University of New York, providing preparation for professional teachers.[76]

The great battle of the second year of his administration occurred over his canal proposal. Here, the radicals rose against the governor. They wanted the surplus revenue of the state, inclusive of the sur-

---

75. Lincoln, 78.

76. Lincoln, 80.

plus profits from the canals, to be used entirely for paying off the state debt, leaving the canals unfinished and unimproved. The Barnburners realized that if the Governor's recommendations would be favorably acted on, the Democratic Party would be committed to this policy so they fought zealously to prevent such action. Robert Dennison, chairman of the state committee on the canals and a leader in the Barnburner movement, prepared a report utterly and scathingly condemning the whole canal system.

Fortunately for Bouck, however, Democratic Assemblyman Horatio Seymour from Utica, a friend and fellow canal commissioner from the construction period, introduced an exhaustive report and bill to carry out the Governor's recommendations.[77] Seymour's report was so well researched and written it became the state's canal policy for the next twenty years.[78] Seymour argued that the State should have "a liberal system of internal improvements, furnishing the elements of and predicated upon a sound financial policy."[79]

Seymour saw a great future for the Erie Canal. He saw a continued increase of the total receipts from the canals and recommended that the surplus revenues of the canal be spent on completing unfinished work and improving the canals already in use. Seymour was among the most effective and eloquent platform orators of the time and presented his case to the legislature. His bill passed 67 to 38 in the Assembly and 17 to 13 in the Senate. The bill provided for the election of the canal commissioners by the people, issuing a loan for $900,000, and for the completion of the proposed improvements of the Erie Canal.[80] Governor Bouck had scored an enormous success with the help of his friend Seymour.

---

77. Horatio Seymour was born in Utica, New York. He served in the New York Assembly from 1842-46, as mayor of Utica (1843), and governor of New York (1853-55 and 1863-65). He also ran as the Democratic candidate for president of the United States in 1860 and 1868. He died on February 12, 1886, in Utica.

78. Seymour's "Canal Report," number 177, comprising seventy-one pages, can be found in *New York Documents, 1844,* VII, 177.

79. Seymour, "Canal Report," 12.

80. Stewart Mitchell. *Horatio Seymour of New York.* Cambridge, Mass.: Harvard University Press, 1938, 76.

Just before the adjournment of the legislature, both conservative and radical Democratic members held a caucus. A bitter fight arose over commending Governor Bouck's administration. A commendation was finally adopted but many of the radicals refused to agree and published a statement to that effect. The Democratic Party had split solidly into two factions and any further cooperation between the two would not take place. Governor Bouck had tried to work together with both sides and was disappointed that he could not bring them together. On a visit to Westchester county in 1843, Governor Bouck felt he had "faithfully discharged the duties which a too partial and indulgent people have devolved upon me." He said he had "erred in some instances, among the various and peculiar duties, and the numerous appointments to office" but he also realized that the office came with tremendous responsibilities and difficulties that many other governors faced with similar results.[81]

* * *

During the summer of 1844, Bouck became worried about his prospects for re-nomination. Silas Wright, New York Senator and a major Martin Van Buren supporter, was being mentioned as a possible replacement for Bouck. Wright said all summer long he was not interested in the position but might be drafted into accepting the nomination. Bouck wrote to his son-in-law:

"I saw a letter from Mr. Wright under the date of 16 Aug. in which he says he cannot be a candidate. I am satisfied he does not wish to be, but it is not certain that he may not consent to be a candidate if proposed by Flagg, etc., his feelings are with them. My friends think he cannot be nominated though he might desire it.

"I should regard the election of Mr. Wright as the restoration of the old Regency, it would be so regarded by my friends, and there is danger that he would feel it in the canvass. It appears to me that I cannot withdraw in order to unite the convention on Wright, though I may be forced to endure the mortification of being rejected by the convention. If Van Buren had been nominated, he would have regarded me as essential to his success, and would have silenced the *Atlas*; but he would have been defeated and probably carried me down with him as in 1840."[82]

---

81. *Albany Evening Atlas*, June 15, 1843.

82. Martin van Buren had campaigned for the presidency in 1844 but lost the nomination to James Polk. Bouck believed that even if

With the election pending, the negative campaigning started all over again. A popular tune of the day promoted Col. Richard Johnson, former vice president under Van Buren, at the expense of Bouck. Johnson sought support for his campaign for president leading up to the Democratic national convention in September of 1844. He was also popular with working class men in the east and had some support in New York State.

Johnson Melodies

Our Johnson boat is now afloat
Just starting from the shore
And to the foreman's chorus note
Responds the dipping oar.
Our songs will sing with happy cheer
And onward many they ring
Till old and young both far and near
Shall all for Johnson sing.

Chorus

We'll vote for neither Van nor Clay
The ball is rolling wide
Our Johnson boat is now afloat
We'll row them down the tide
For Bouck we ne'er again will row
His boat has sprung a leak
He's up "salt river" soon will go
To old Vly Summit's peak
But we will, like true hearted men,
Row faster than before
And pull with all our might and main
'Till he is run ashore.[83]

Gov. Bouck's political fortune turned at the Democratic presidential national convention in Baltimore in September, 1844. Martin van Buren was the likely nominee for the party going into the convention. However, when the convention was over, Van Buren lost

Van Buren had won the nomination, he would have lost the election in November, just like the election of 1840.

83. Bouck papers.

the nomination and James Polk was selected. Before the convention, Van Buren had managed to bring both factions of the New York Democratic Party into an uneasy alliance and both sides had shown support for another Bouck term. But Van Buren's defeat had broken the thin wafer sealing the factions together in New York. If Bouck were to stay in the race, the party would become hopelessly divided and the state would go to the Whigs. The Whigs would take New York and probably install their nominee, Henry Clay, as president. Since Polk received the nomination, Silas Wright became the only man who was acceptable to both sides of the party for governor. Wright would make the difference between victory and defeat in New York and the thirty-six electoral votes the Democrats needed in the presidential race.[84]

Just before the New York State Democratic convention for governor, Wright agreed to let his name go before the convention. There was pressure on Bouck to retire but he refused. He would take his case to the convention floor. At the convention in Syracuse in September, 1844, Bouck was defeated for renomination. The vote was Silas Wright 95, Bouck 30. The convention closed by giving thanks to Governor Bouck and Lt. Governor Dickinson, "for their faithful administration of the various and responsible duties committed to their charge. Coming into power when the financial affairs of the government had become involved in embarrassment and depression, in consequence of maladministration of their predecessors, they devoted themselves with universal zeal and assiduity to their various duties, especially to the task of restoring the faith and resources of this great commonwealth."[85]

Bouck was afterwards quite bitter towards Wright, although he did not consider the man a villain, but rather a pathetic stooge of the party manipulators. Bouck commented, "The secret of the whole matter is that Mr. Wright was the willing agent of Mr. Van Buren and a small circle of his peculiar friends who pounced upon me like so many bloodhounds."[86] During the campaign, Bouck did not lend his support to the party's nominee. He opposed Wright's nomination and especially disliked the way Wright entered the campaign. John Staat, a life-long friend of Bouck, commented, "I regret very

84. Garraty, 304.

85. *Albany Morning Atlas,* Sept. 4, 1844.

86. Bouck papers.

much that he has been brought forward at this time and still more that he did not positively decline the nomination when he knew, as you say, that you would be his competition. His acceptance under the circumstances you mention reflect no credit upon him. The foul breath of calamity cannot sully your reputation."[87]

Silas Wright was elected governor by over ten thousand votes in the fall election.

The last appointment Governor Bouck would make before his term expired was to fill the U.S. Senate seat vacated by governor-elect Wright[88]. (In fact, Bouck had two senate seats to fill, as Sen. Nathaniel Tallmadge resigned his seat to become governor of the territory of Wisconsin.) There was some talk that Bouck would nominate himself for one of the seats, his son saying, "I have heard your name much in connection with the place to be vacated by Mr. Wright."[89] But Bouck knew his opponents would never approve the nomination. In the end, Lt. Governor Dickinson and state Senator Henry Foster were nominated. Both nominees were, of course, subjected to harsh attacks in the press and in the legislature for their association with Bouck. Dickinson was finally approved but Foster did not receive legislative approval.

Shortly before the close of the administration of Governor Bouck, the public peace was disturbed by renewed disturbances on manorial lands. This matter involved the leasehold rights of several large landowners to collect quit-rent from the tenants on their estates. The 'anti-renters', the protesting tenant farmers, called for an end to the anachronistic system of patroonship. Bouck was a staunch ally of the anti-renters and in every way attempted to help them.

---

87. Bouck papers.

88. Bouck learned the political game in his two years as governor. Wright did not have to give up his seat as senator right after the election but Bouck convinced him that New York needed representation in Washington during the fall congressional sessions, which Wright did not plan to attend. Wright agreed without giving it much thought and wrote out his resignation right there on the spot; he could have waited until January to resign. Bouck immediately appointed two of his Hunker allies to the senate seats, thereby giving the Hunkers the two seats for the next six years.

89. Bouck papers.

His aid took the shape of delaying law enforcement attempts to evict the tenants for their refusal to pay rent. In several instances, he would not allow the militia to be used to quell demonstrations. His main hope was that the farmers could organize and elect enough legislators who then would vote to break up the estates by legal means.

However, demonstrations and disturbances of the anti-renters reached such a crescendo that the general situation warranted being called a war. Bands of anti-rent tenants had armed and disguised themselves as Indians and refused to pay any more rent. The land-owners turned to the governor for assistance but Bouck refused; he would not use the militia or law enforcement agencies (sheriffs) to collect rent. Bouck took the matter into his own hands and met with the anti-renters in West Sand Lake on August 10, 1844, to try to mediate the situation. He worked out a truce where the tenants would not riot anymore as long as the sheriffs would leave them alone. The tenants agreed to pay the rents until they could elect their own men to the next legislature and affect change through new laws abolishing the feudal lands.

The meeting calmed the situation for the time being. Bouck was viewed as a hero to the farmers and the farmers congratulated themselves that "all the governor lacked of being an Indian was the calico." But the landowners and the Barnburner press sharply criticized Bouck for "infusing a sense of confidence in the ranks of the insurgents by meeting to negotiate with them on their own ground."[90]

The truce did not last long and the situation continued to worsen. Despite all the editorials and highly colored accounts of "Indian outrages" that filled the press, Bouck did not waver in his determination to deny the landowners the use of state troops as rent collectors. Political opponents naturally made capital of the governor's stubbornness. Not only the Whigs but also the Barnburner faction were delighted to be handed such ammunition so close to the November elections.

Finally, in December of 1844, official papers of the Columbia county sheriff were forcibly taken from him and burned. At a meeting of anti-renters, a young man was shot dead. Bouck had to take action and he issued a proclamation offering a five hundred dollar reward "paid to persons who shall give information resulting in the

---

90. *Albany Daily Argus*, August 20, 1844.

conviction of those who have disturbed the peace, resisted the execution of the laws, or committed violence on the sheriff."[91]

Bouck consulted with state officers and governor-elect Wright and they decided to order an armed force to assist Columbia county authorities in maintaining order and enforcing the law. The demonstration was put down. This was Bouck's last official action. The new Governor, Silas Wright, would side with the landowners and use the militia to collect rent. The leaders of the anti-renters were arrested and thrown into jail. Their houses and property were sold at public auction. The troubles would continue for several more years until the power of the landowners was finally broken as more and more anti-renters were elected to state office. They passed laws which abolished the feudal estates and the leasing of agricultural lands. Never again in New York State could anyone hold large acres of land in bondage forever. And these were just the reforms Bouck argued for during his term as governor!

Bouck expressed his opinion of the new administration often in the months to come. In a letter to his son dated January 1845, Bouck lamented that "a more proscriptive, intolerant and illiberal set of men never congregated together before."[92] Bouck however, left office optimistic about the future of the state and the democratic principles of the union: He served in the public eye for over forty years and always believed in the leading principles of the Democratic Party espoused by Thomas Jefferson. Bouck believed that the "highest and most sacred political duty was to maintain the integrity and harmony of the Union." He believed that politicians should do nothing "inconsistent with the welfare of the whole."[93] Bouck always served to benefit his fellow citizens. He stood up for what he believed in even if sometimes it was not the most popular stand.

Some people have written that Bouck was not reelected because he was not a good governor, but one can see that Bouck had accomplished much to benefit the people of New York.

He just lost support in the splintered Democratic Party and became a casualty of the infighting between the Barnburners and the Hunkers. The next seven governors of New York State—including Silas Wright—were also not reelected to a second term.

---

91. Bouck Papers.

92. Bouck Papers.

93. *Albany Morning Atlas,* Sept. 2, 1844.

Governor Bouck, from a glass plate in the Mark Sullivan collection.

6. Elder Statesman

In 1846, a convention was called by the New York State Legislature to revise the state constitution. Governor Bouck's old friends and neighbors choose him to be a delegate. He did not particularly want to be a delegate, as he wrote to a friend in December 1845, prior to the convention:

> *The idea of being a candidate for popular suffrage appears to me very forbidding. My impressions are decidedly against it and nothing could induce me to consent but an unequivocal and distant expression that it is desired by the people. Aside from my repugnance to be a candidate, I have several good friends in the county who may desire the place. I regard the democratic party as broken to pieces and entirely alienated feelings and differing widely on principles on state and national politics.*
> *Wm Bouck[94]*

Bouck reluctantly attended and served as chairman of the committee on the elective franchise during the convention. As chairman of the committee, he authored a report recommending some revisions of the qualifications for voting and holding office which were accepted by the convention. Senators and assemblymen henceforth were to be elected each from a single district, an arrangement which made legislators more directly responsible to their constitutes. The term of senator was set at two years, of assemblyman at one year. And all state offices, including judgeships, were made elective.

Bouck made one other suggestion at the convention liberalizing the suffrage. He suggested the convention consider allowing blacks virtually equal rights with the white electors. But this did not pass. In the end, the blacks' right to vote was dependent upon a residence requirement and upon the payment of a property tax.

During the convention in June, 1846, he was appointed by President James Polk to be assistant treasurer of the City of New York, a position he held until May, 1849. The appointment did not particularly set well with the Wright administration. Bouck was still viewed the head of the opposition and got "crowned king of the sub-treasury. There may be another man in the State who would be more distasteful to the democracy than Bouck, but if there is, I do not

---

94. Bouck papers.

know him," quipped John O'Sullivan, editor of the *Democratic Review* and a strong supporter of Wright.[95] Bouck discharged the duties of the office at a time when the United States was at war with Mexico serving with great integrity, until he was removed by President Zachary Taylor. Then, he returned to his island farm in the valley of the Schoharie to enjoy retirement. John Staats, a life-long friend commented:

> *Sir,*
>
> *You express your intentions of retiring from your present situation to your home on the banks of the Schoharie. Among some of my earliest recollections is that of having visited that 'sweet spot' in company with my father. To my boyish eye, it looked like paradise. May the blessing of God rest upon you in your retirement.*
>
>

John Staats, Sept. 15, 1847[96]

Bouck's son had tried to convince him to keep active and remain in Albany, saying, "I should advise you by no means to go to Schoharie. I have no doubts you can get a situation suitable to your present position. Your position now before the people is of high standing and influence and by returning to Schoharie, you will soon be forgotten. You should not allow your enemies an easy triumph."[97] His son also talked about the cold Schoharie county winters and the idea of going south for the winter: "I have made further inquiries about Cuba and southern places where you might go and spend the winter. I inquired the expense of boarding in Havana and it would cost you hardly nothing and you will be treated pretty well."[98]

Governor Bouck continued his correspondence during his retirement years on his farm at Bouck's Island.[99] He spent many hours

---

95. Letter of John O'Sullivan to Samuel J. Tilden, editor of the *New York Morning News*. Tilden papers, New York Public Library.

96. Bouck papers.

97. Bouck papers.

98. Bouck papers.

99. Many of the letters Bouck received are housed at Cornell University. Unfortunately, the letters Bouck wrote have been lost or are scattered around in the country in various historical collections.

each day writing to his friends and political allies, talking about the old times and about the current political events of the day.

Bouck also received requests for recommendations and letters of introductions. One came from Dewitt Roberts, the son of Nathan S. Roberts, Bouck's friend from the Erie Canal days. Dewitt was looking for a letter of recommendation and he mentioned the ill health of his father. Governor Bouck immediately sent off this particularly touching letter to his old friend from the canal days:

> *My dear sir,*
>
> *Very often have I thought of you and the many trying scenes through which we passed on the Erie Canal. Impressions have been made on my mind which will not be erased while time and memory remains. I often think of your great fidelity and devotion to the public work, your personal convenience and comfort was always a secondary consideration. Very few of the pioneers on the canals are now alive. I am the only commissioner who was in commission on the completion of the canal in 1825 and you I believe the only chief engineer. My health is good. I have done with active politics and am a looker on in the quiet enjoyment of domestic life.*
>
> *Wm C. Bouck, Fultonham Dec. 24, '51.*[100]

One of the issues Bouck wrote about and discussed in his correspondence was the issue of slavery. He foresaw trouble on the horizon if the issue was not resolved. John Staats wrote to Bouck in March 1859:

"Sir, I begin to think and fear that it will be impossible to keep up a union between the northern and southern democracy. The south is becoming too outrageously exacting and so violently denunciatory in its language of northern democrats. It appears to me that our southern brethrens are determined to secede from the union. This question of slavery is a fearful one and only omniscience can tell what consequences will grow out of it."[101]

* * *

The state census of 1855 gives us a picture of Governor Bouck's farm. It was being run by his son Charles. The frame house was val-

---

100. Bouck papers.
101. Bouck papers.

ued at $2,000; William C. Bouck was listed as a farmer, 69 years old, his wife Catherine, 68. The farm was in the first election district of the town of Fulton. Thirty-five families lived in log houses in the district. There were one cooper shop, three shoemakers, ten sawmills, one waggoner, one barrel and firkin factory, one harness maker, five blacksmiths, one union church, one inn, two retail stores and four schools.

The farm consisted of 230 improved acres, 150 unimproved acres, 75 plowed acres, 70 acres in pasture and 40 acres of meadow. There were 25 tons of hay, 16 bushels of grass seed, 35 acres of winter wheat (150 bushels harvested), 30 acres of oats (900 bushels harvested), 10 acres of corn (500 bushels harvested), one-half acre of potatoes (75 bushels harvested), 75 bushels of apples, 75 bushels of carrots valued at $25.00, tobacco (received 5½ cents a pound), cattle—three under one year old, 14 over a year, two cows, two working oxen, one cow killed for beef, two cows milked and 250 lbs. of butter, nine horses, 21 swine and 21 sheep. Four fleeces (13 pounds of wool), special manure, 2,000 lbs. of gypsum, 18 yards of fulled cloth, 6 yards of flannel cloth, and brooms were listed under other articles of domestic manufacture.

Four years after the census and at age 73, Governor Bouck was taken ill.

N.Y. Feb. 1859

Dear Father,

I cannot express my feelings when I received a short letter from Dr. Danforth stating your illness and situation. Joseph leaves today and I have given him express directions, that if you are in danger or seriously ill, to send to Albany for me and telegraph from there. I shall pray earnestly that a kind and good God will spare you yet awhile so your numerous friends who love you much, or at least until I can again see you. But if it is otherwise, I pray that we may meet in the home prepared for us by our blessed savior.

Very affectionately yours
C M Bouck[102]

---

102. Edward Sanford Ronan, "The Administration of Gov. William C. Bouck," in *Quarterly Bulletin of the Schoharie County Historical Society* VII, 2, April 1943, 12.

The *Schoharie Republican* announced on April 21, 1859, that the governor had passed away:

Death of Ex-Gov. Wm. C. Bouck

At his residence in the 74th year of his age at 5 o'clock AM the 19th inst. The Hon. William C. Bouck passed from the scenes of earth to those of eternity. Though the age of the deceased and his feeble health the past three months were admonitory of the "sad hour's approach." The event enshrouds a community in gloom. Still there is that in his life of integrity and virtue, which is better than "the blood of sacrifice," and which sheds a halo of peace and hope over the desolate circle, and tells with all the pathos of eloquence, the magnitude of the loss, and the grandeur of life, the memory of which is unsullied and co-existed with the veneration for virtue. Of the positions of confidence and honor held by the deceased—the rigid faithfulness with which their respective duties were discharged—of the many virtues which adorned alike his private and public life, we cannot now speak; a more facile pen than ours is requisite to pay them their merited tribute. His obsequies will be attended at his late residence in Fultonham, on Thursday, the 21st inst. at 1 o'clock PM by Rev. Dr. Lintner.[103]

The legislature adopted resolutions of respect.

In the senate, April 19th, Mr. Diven moved the following, which was adopted unanimously, after a brief eulogy on the public life and character and private virtues of the deceased:

---

103. Rev. Dr. George Ames Lintner was born in Minden, Montgomery County, in February 1796. He graduated from Union College in 1817 and two years later was regularly ordained pastor of the Evangelical Lutheran Churches of Schoharie, Middleburgh and Cobleskill. He rose to eminence as a divine, and in 1835 was honored by the degree of doctor of divinity. He was also very active in the Lutheran church hierarchy, serving as president of the General Synod of the United States, 1841-1845, and as author and editor of many church publications. His funeral address is found in Appendix D.

*Resolved, in the death of the Honorable William C. Bouck,
the country has lost an enlightened statesman, society an honest
man, and the Christian religion a firm supporter. That with our
regrets at the loss to the people of the State and Country, we
mingle our sympathy with the bereaved family of our late distinguished fellow-citizen, and its members extend our unfeigned
and heartfelt condolence.*

*Resolved, that a copy of these resolutions be sent to the fam-
ily of the deceased.*

Governor Bouck was buried in the family cemetery on Bouck's
Island and later moved to the Middleburgh cemetery.

Two years later, Bouck's widow, Catherine, passed away.

*Died, at her residence in Fultonham, on the 19th of Aug.,
1861, Catherine, wife of the late Ex-Governor William C.
Bouck, in the 75th year of her age. Mrs. Bouck was married in
the year 1807. In 1808, she and her husband united to the
Evangelical Lutheran Church of Schoharie, under the ministry
of Rev. Dr. Wackenhagen, and for upwards of fifty years she
sustained an unblemished Christian character. In her last illness, which was short, she evinced full submission to the will of
her heavenly Father, and died full of the comforts and consola-
tions of that faith which she had professed for so many years.
Her loss is lamented by a large circle of friends, who will cher-
ish her memory with respect and affection.*

Schoharie Patriot, Aug. 29, 1861

&

Epilogue

William C. Bouck saw many changes during his life. Travel was at first on foot over Indian trails and then by horse and carriage, and wagon, over dirt, plank and toll roads and through covered bridges. He saw drovers take their animals to market by foot. By the end of his life, travel was by canals, railroads and steamships.

Dean Harry J. Carman of Columbia University summed up Bouck's life in these words: "He was regular and frugal in his habits and was blessed through life with good health. The official honors bestowed upon him he owed not so much to the backing of powerful friends as to his native talents and strength of character." Bouck himself described his strengths and weakness, always believing in his caring and understanding nature would benefit his fellow man: "The difference in the position of Mr. Van Buren and myself is this—he is strong with politicians but weak with the people—my strength is with the people, who are seldom heard in matters relating to nominations and public good."[104]

Many historians of Bouck's time have spoken very poorly of William Bouck. They looked down on him for his poor education, his rural upbringing, his strong Dutch accent, and maybe even his unexciting personality. However, looking at his accomplishments as a whole, Bouck compares to any of the men of his times. His accomplishments on the Erie Canal and the canal system changed the course of history in the United States. His two years as governor were stormy but still, he pushed through needed legislation, which improved life in the Empire State. William Bouck was underestimated by many people his whole life. "That Mr. Bouck possesses a large share of good sense, prudence, and discretion, is evident to all who are acquainted with him. Indeed, a moment's reflection will convince any person that a man brought up in the interior country, in a secluded neighborhood, without the benefit of a liberal education, or in fact much reading, who should for thirty years, without the aid of powerful friends and relatives, continue to rise from one grade to another, until, by the voluntary suffrages of his fellow citizens, he should become governor of a state containing nearly three

---

104. Bouck papers.

million people, must not only have been master of an excellent address, but have possessed great native mental power."[105]

Not possessed of rhetorical ability or personal magnetism, Bouck would probably have not believed it possible for him to have the varied career that he enjoyed. Looking back on his career, he could say justly he had been honest to himself and served the public well.

ଔ ଔ ଔ

---

105. Jenkins, 345.

Appendix A: Bouck Family Tree

Ancestors of William C. Bouck
b. 7 Jan. 1786, d. 19 Apr. 1859

1. Parents
F. Christian Bouck, b. 18 Oct. 1753, d. 1836
M. Margaret Borst, b. 17 Oct. 1762. m. 23 Nov. 1785

2. Grandparents
PGF. Johan Wilhelmus Bouck, b. 4 Jan. 1712, d. 7 Feb. 1780
PGM. Anna Elisabeth Krausler (Crisler), b. 9 June 1721
MGF. Johan Joost Borst, b. 4 Jan 1730, d. 30m July 1784
MGM. Catharina Fuchs (Fox), b. 28 Aug. 1714, m. 10 Oct., 1758?

3. Great-Grandparents
Parents of Johan Wilhelm Bouck: Christian Bauch, d. 17 Dec. 1752 and Anna Dorotha, b. 1679 d. 19 Jan 1747

Parents of Anna Elisabeth Krausler: Adam Krausler, m. 13 July 1710 Maria Brant

Parents of Johan Joost Borst: Jacob H. Borst, d. 1757, m. Maria Barbara Bellinger, b. 1686, d. 3 Aug. 1753

Parents of Catharina Fuchs: Johann Philipp Fuchs.

Descendants of William C. Bouck and Catherine Lawyer
William C. Bouck, b. 7 Jan. 1786, d. 19 April 1859
Catherine Lawyer, b. 1787, d. 1861
m. 23 Nov. 1785

1. James Madison, 1808-1865
2. Joseph William, b. 27 Oct. 1809, d. 1886
3. Margaret, b. 23 Nov. 1811, d. 1837?
4. Anne Eve, b. 29 Dec. 1814, m. Lyman Sanford 1 Nov. 1837, d. 19 Feb. 1890
5. Christian W., b. 1816
6. Christina, b. 14 May 1818, d. 1836?

7. Catherine, b. 10 July 1820, m. George Danforth 19 May 1852, d. 1899
8. Caroline, b. 1822?, m. Volney Danforth 4 Oct. 1842
9. Elizabeth, b. 13 July 1825, d. 1826
10. Gabriel,[106] b. 16 Dec. 1827
11. Charles,[107] b. 8 Sept. 1829, m. Juliett Best 1859

∞

---

106. Gabriel was a graduate of Union College and soon after moved to Oshkosh, Wisconsin. He later became a colonel in the Civil War, a member of Congress and an attorney general in Wisconsin. He was a colorful character with a vigorous personality and a forceful expression of his independent views.

107. Charles served in the New York State Assembly in the year 1878.

Appendix B: The Sauerkraut Message

Dr. Sylvanus Palmer (also known as Peter Paradox in the literary world) was the author of the article. Dr. Palmer was born near Canastota Station on August 4, 1804. He was a teacher in his early years and then studied medicine in the office of Dr. Shepherd, at Lawyersville, around 1822. He set up his own practice in that town in 1825 after receiving his license. "No more agreeable conversationalist could be found than the doctor, and he was ever ready to be amusing and instructive." He died suddenly at his home in October, 1880.

Reading the message, it must be remembered that it is written in low Dutch brogue, and the English 'e' should be pronounced as English 'a.'

"Veller Shitizens,

.....I vint dat some untankvul peebles crumples mooch at de apuntance of offish in mine own vamily. Now I puts dis to your own gase, chendlemen. Yor wen offish triple tro' mine vinchers, it ov coorse op dem wat ish nearesht py virsht trobs; ant wat coult you to selbst? Maar, more als dish, I pe not alone to plame, any how; vor Hansjie Dyler kifs mein poys mooch offish—mooch shwee botatoes ant topack, vrom hees firchinary varm; ant we gan't helb it. Maar dey pe like de Intian's cun: dey gosht more ash dey gome to. Dey pe very coot, iv we coult dem in beace ead. Maar it pe, we pe in a guantary, vor I all mein roeletjies and all mein worsht expects vrom Mr. Van Pooren. Zo here pe I, pedwix 2 vires. Ant zo it ish you zee. Fery many of der peebles exbextsh me out to gome in mein messitch vor Mr. Van Pooren; ant dere he sit, selbst, mit de water running town from pote gorners of hees mout, waiting vor some sh ibbers of sourkrout vrom mein daple clot, dat ish mein messitch. Ant wat gan I, a boor varmer, to?? Dere pesure shtant I, vumplin mit pote hants in mein mout, vull of shmoking hot firschinny taters, in cread acony to see de one of mein poys bainfully mumpling a whole beg of hot kinterhook worsht, de water a shtreaming pote hees eyes out; and an oder poy so shtuft mit firchinny topack, dat de schmoke roll hees mout, hees nose, and oder blaces out!! Ant dere, petwigsht me ant mein poys, sit Hansjie Dyler too, mit pote hants op hees pelly, pegause he ish mit de Botts drupplet; waiting to see if I no sourkrout for him trob; hees wan goaxin eye shmile mite hobe; wile

67

die oder, fery toudvul, ant treatening, ish trawed, ish trawed town unter hees gin, mit a shcowl targer as sefen donder glouts."

Translation:

I think that some unthankful people grumble much at the abundance of office in my family. Now I put this to your case, gentlemen. For when offices dribble through my fingers, it is of course on them that is nearest by the first drops; and what could you do yourself?? Maar, more than this, I be not alone to blame, anyhow; for John Tyler gives my boys much office—much sweet potatoes and tobacco, from his Virginia farm; and we can't help it. Maar, they be like the Indian corn: they have more than they come to. They be very good, if we could eat them in peace. Maar as it be, we be in a quandary, for I expect all my royalties and all my wurst from Mr. Van Buren. So here be I, between two fires. And so it is you see. Very much of the people expect me to come out in my message for Mr. Van Buren. And there he sit, himself, with the water running down from both corners of his mouth, waiting for some slivers of sauerkraut from my table cloth, that is my message. And what can I, a poor farmer do?? There I stand, fumbling with both hands in my mouth, for full of smoking hot Virginia taters, in great agony to see one of my boys painfully mumbling a whole bag of hot Kinderhook wurst, the water streaming out of both his eyes; and another boy so stuffed with Virginia tobacco, that the smoke roll out of his mouth, his nose, and other places!!! And there, between me and my boys, sits John Tyler too, with both hands on his belly, because he is with the bots droplet, waiting to see if I drop no sauerkraut for him; his one coaxing eye smiles with hope; while the other, very doubtful, and threatening, is drawn down under his chin, with a scowl darker than seven dozengrunt.

಼

Appendix C: "On the Death of W. C. Bouck"

Rev. Dr. George Lintner preached the following funeral sermon at the Bouck homestead on April 21, 1859:

The subject we have been considering addresses a general application, but it commands itself more particularly to our attention on this solemn occasion when we have met here to mourn the loss of a distinguished citizen and valued friend whose life and death may be regarded as a practical illustration of the sentiments expressed in our text.

William C. Bouck was born on the seventh day of January 1786. In early life, he had not the advantages of education with which most of our public men were favored. He received only a common school education but he was early trained to those sound religious principles and habits of honesty and thorough mental disciple which gave so much strength and energy to his character in his subsequent career. He had naturally a strong will, well balanced mind, which was carefully cultivated and enriched by the treasures of practical observation and experience. He was a self-educated and self-made man. He formed his character on those principles of religion and virtue which can alone render us useful in the world. And upon those principles with the divine blessing he relied for success. He had a great desire to render himself useful, to serve his country and do good with the gifts and talents stowed upon him. And we have reason to believe that he made this desire the governing principle of his life and to this great end, all his energies were dedicated. How far he succeeded in this purpose is now a matter of history. He successfully filled the offices of member of the assembly, senate, canal commissioner, and governor of this state. Besides these he also held several important and responsible offices and in the religious and benevolent institutions of the church with which he stood connected. He was one of the founders of the Hartwick Seminary in 1815 and was President of that institution, the only office he held at the time of his death. He was also formerly President of the Danube Missionary Society of the Lutheran Church in the State of New York and President of the Temperance Union of this county. His name is recorded among the statesmen of our county who have filled her high places of trust and responsibility and no one has ever acquitted himself with greater fidelity to the trusts that were reposed in him. In all the high official stations which he filled, not the slightest doubt ever rested on his character. He discharged all his duties faithfully and honorable and retired from every office which he held with the confidence of the public and credit to himself. He was an honest, upright, faithful public servant and no man, not even his political opponents, could ever charge him with having violated or neglected any of his duties of his several trusts.

This is high commendation but it is due to our departed friend. It is a praise that but few of our humble men can claim but it will be readily and cheerfully conceded by all who knew him.

He had a very discerning and discriminating mind. He was a careful and judicious observer of the characters and conduct of man. But few men could judge as readily and correctly as he did on moral and political questions affecting the public interest. No man ever professed the confidence of the community in which he lived more generally and fully than he did. He was consulted at all times and on all subjects and so highly were his opinions and counsels valued, that they were most always followed. He was a man of sound judgment and strong practical wisdom whose advice could be safely followed in all cases requiring careful discrimination and discreet action. He was always ready to labor for the public good and seemed anxious to promote the benevolent enterprises of the day.

Our lamented friend possessed many excellent traits of character for which he was honored while living and will be remembered when dead. But his crowning excellence was his humble, genuine piety. He loved religion from an inward conviction of its divine power in his own heart and made it the governing principle of all of his actions. I do not say that he was entirely free from the imperfections of our fallen and sinful nature. That would be attributing to him a degree of excellence unattainable in this world of sin and temptation. But I do say that in all the public duties, cares and perplexities of office, he maintained an unblemished Christian character. He never lost sight of his duty to that God and Savior to whom he owed all his qualifications for usefulness in this world and his hope of happiness in that which is to come. He was a true Christian and it was this trait in his character which added so much to his other excellent qualities as a statesman and filled him more than any thing else for the high and honorable stations which in the providence of God he was called to fill. He drank in the spirit of Christianity at the fountain of grace and from that living fountain he derived wisdom and strength to qualify him for all the duties of life. It was this that rendered him so faithful and trustworthy in all his public and private relations and in this lay the secret of his power and success in very enterprise for the good of his fellow creatures.

His mark on earth is done. His labors are ended and he has begun to reap that eternal reward which the Lord has promised his servants. While we commute his remains to the tomb and mourn over his departure, we rejoice to know that our loss is his gain. We bless God that in his life and death he has given us another illustration of the excellence and power of religion which can carry us with honor and usefulness through life and muster comfort and consolation to us in death."[108]

&

---

108. Lintner family papers, box 3, folder 6.

Appendix D: Bouckville

From *History of Chenango and Madison Counties, New York* by James H. Smith, D. Mason & Co., Syracuse, N.Y., 1880.

Bouckville is situated near the center of the west border, on the line of the Utica, Clinton and Binghamton Railroad and the Chenango Canal, which passes through a deep cutting at this place. It contains one church (Methodist Episcopal), a district school (built about 1876, at a cost of some $1,600), one hotel (known as the White House, and kept by William Edgarton), one store, a steam saw-mill and cheese box factory, two extensive cider mills, two blacksmith shops (Chauncey Clark and Columbus Lewis), a shoe shop (D. W. Smith), and about fifty dwellings. It is six miles from Hamilton and two from Madison.

Bouckville has enjoyed the distinction of various cognomens. It was first known as McClure Settlement, from the McClure tavern located there, and contemporaneously as The Hook. Later it was christened Johnsville, at a drunken carousal, in honor of John Edgarton, the first settler on its site. When the post-office was established, it received its present name, in honor of William C. Bouck, who was then Canal Commissioner (1837).

ജ ജ ജ

Sources

Adams, Samuel Hopkins, *Erie Canal*. New York: Random House, 1953.

―――, *Grandfather Stories*. New York: Random House, 1947.

Albany *Daily Argus*, 1840-44.

Albany *Evening Atlas*, 1840-44.

Albany *Evening Journal*, 1840-44.

Albany *Microscope*, 1840-44.

Albany *Morning Atlas*, 1844.

Alexander, Holmes, *The American Talleyrand: The Career and Contemporaries of Martin Van Buren, Eighth President*. New York: Harper & Brothers, 1935.

Andrist, Ralph K., *The Erie Canal*. New York: Harper & Row, 1964.

Baker, Kirby L., *Farmer Governor of New York*, unpublished thesis, Harvard University, 1957.

Beach, Allen C., *The Centennial Celebrations of the State of New York*. Albany, N.Y.: 1879.

Beekman, Dow, *Historical Sketch of the Life of Governor William C. Bouck of Schoharie County*. Cobleskill, N.Y.: *Cobleskill Index*, 1937.

Benson, Lee, *Concept of Jacksonian Democracy, New York as a Test Case*. Princeton, N.J.: University Press, 1961.

Bouck, Johannes, pension application R1053. National Archives and Records Administration, *Records of Military Pensions, Revolutionary War*. Record Group M408. Washington, D.C.

Bouck, William, *William C. Bouck papers*, 1727-1866. Division of Rare and Manuscript Collections, Cornell University Library, Ithaca, N.Y.

Brockway, Beman, *Fifty Years in Journalism Embracing Recollections and Personal Experiences*. Watertown, N.Y.: Daily Times Printing, 1891.

Brunger, Eric, *The Grand Canal New York's First Thruway*. Buffalo, N.Y.: Buffalo and Erie County Historical Society, 1964.

Chalmers, Harvey, *The Birth of the Erie Canal*. New York: Bookman Associates, 1960.

Christman, Henry, *Tin Horns and Calico*. New York: Henry Holt and Co., 1945.

Clinton, De Witt. *The Canal Policy of the State of New York.* Albany, N.Y.: Bosford, 1821.

Colden, Cadwallader D., *Memoir Prepared at the Request of Committee of the Common Council of the City of New York, and Presented to the Mayor of the City, at the Celebration of the Completion of the New York Canals.* New York, 1825.

Condon, George E., *Stars in the Water: The Story of the Erie Canal.* Garden City, N.Y.: Doubleday & Co., 1974.

Donovan, Herbert D.A., *Barnburners.* New York: New York University Press, 1925.

Eaton, Moses, *Five Years on the Erie Canal: An Account of Some of the Most Striking Scenes and Incidents.* Utica, N.Y.: Bennett, Backus & Hawley, 1845.

Ellis, David M.; Frost, James A.; Syrett, Harold C. and Carman, Harry J., *Short History of New York State.* Ithaca, N.Y.: Cornell University Press, 1957.

Finch, Roy G., *Story of the New York State Canals.* Albany, N.Y.: J.B. Lyon Company, 1925.

Fitzsimmons, Neal, *The Reminiscences of John B. Jervis, Engineer of the Old Croton.* Syracuse, N.Y.: Syracuse University Press, 1971.

Garraty, John A., *Silas Wright.* New York: Columbia University Press, 1949.

Hammond, J.D., *History of Political Parties in the State of N.Y.* Albany, N.Y.: Hall & Dickson, 1842.

———, *Life and Times of Silas Wright.* Syracuse, N.Y.: Hall & Dickson, 1848.

———, *Political History of N.Y.* Albany, N.Y.: Hall & Dickson, 1852.

Harlow, Alvin F., *Old Towpaths: The Story of the American Canal Era.* Port Washington, N.Y.: Kennikat Press, 1926.

Hedrick, Ulysses Prentiss, *History of Agriculture in the State of New York.* New York: Hill and Wang, 1933.

Hepburn, A. Barton, *Artificial Waterways and Commercial Development with a History of the Erie Canal.* New York: Macmillan Co., 1909.

Hinman, Marjory B., *Daniel Dickinson Defender of the Constitution.* Windsor, N.Y.: Heart of Lakes, 1987.

Jenkins, John S., *History of Political Parties in the State of New York.* Auburn, N.Y: Derby & Miller, 1846

————, *Life of Silas Wright Late Governor of the State of New York.* Auburn, N.Y.: Alden & Markham, Publishers, 1847.

————, *Lives of the Governors of the State of New York.* Auburn, N.Y: Derby & Miller, 1851.

Journal of the Assembly of the State of New York.

Knittel, Walter Allen, *Early Eighteenth Century Palatine Immigration.* Baltimore, Md., 1970.

Kubik, Dorothy. *A Free Soil—A Free People: The Anti-rent War in Delaware County, New York.* Fleishmann, N.Y.: Purple Mountain Press, 1997.

Larkin, F. Daniel, *New York State Canals A Short History.* Fleischmanns, N.Y.: Purple Mountain Press, 1998.

Lawson, Dorris Moore, *Nathan Roberts, Erie Canal Engineer.* Utica, N.Y.: North Country Books, Inc., 1997.

Lincoln, Charles Z., ed., *Messages from the Governors.* Albany, N.Y.: J.B. Lyon, 1909, vol. IV.

Lintner Family Papers. *Journal of Rev. Dr. George A. Lintner, 1839-1871.* New York State Library, Manuscripts and Special Collections. Albany, New York. Call number SC13168.

Lynch, Denis T., *An Epoch and a Man: Martin Van Buren and his Times.* New York: Horace Liveright, 1929.

Meadowcroft, Enid L., *We Were There at the Opening of the Erie Canal.* New York: Grosset and Dunlap, 1958.

Miller, Nathan, *The Enterprise of a Free People: Aspects of Economic Development in New York During the Canal Period, 1792-1838.* Ithaca, N.Y.: Cornell University Press, 1962.

Mitchell, Stewart, *Horatio Seymour of New York.* Cambridge, Mass. Harvard University Press, 1938.

Murlin, Edgar L., *New York Redbook.* Albany, N.Y., 1900.

New York *Daily News,* 1859.

New York *Daily Post,* 1859.

New York State Agricultural Society, executive committee minutes, Oct. 26, 1841.

New York State Archives and Records Administration, *The Mighty Chain: A Guide to Canal Records in the New York State Archives.* Albany, N.Y., 1992.

Niven, John, *Martin Van Buren: The Romantic Age of American Politics.* New York: Oxford University Press, 1983.

Noyes, Marion F., *History of Schoharie County.* Richmondville, N.Y.: Richmondville Phoenix, 1964.

O'Sullivan, John, to Samuel J. Tilden, editor of the *New York Morning News*. Tilden papers, New York Public Library.

Palatine Society, Inc., *Palatines of New York State*. Johnstown, N.Y., 1953.

Paradox, Peter, *The Paradox Papers: A Copy of Original Humorous Articles including a reprint of the Old Dutch Legislative Sour Krout (sic) Message Number Two*. Albany, N.Y.: Joel Munsell, Printers, 1873.

Porteus, John, *William C. Bouck, Governor From Schoharie*. Schoharie, N.Y.: Schoharie County Historical Society, 1987.

Priest, Josiah, *Traits of the Revolution, With Stories of Hunters in the New Countries and other Curious Matters of Truth*. Langsingburgh, N.Y.: W.B. Harkness, Printers, 1840.

Roberts, Nathan, *Personal Memoirs*. Canastota, N.Y. *Bee Journal*, vol. 52, Feb. 17, 1906 through May 26, 1906.

Ronan, Edward Sanford, "The Administration of Gov. William C. Bouck," *Quarterly Bulletin of the Schoharie County Historical Society*, vol. VII, 2, April 1943, 3-12.

Roscoe, William E., *History of Schoharie County with Illustrations and Biographical Sketches of Some of its Prominent Men and Pioneers*. Syracuse, N.Y.: D. Mason & Co., 1882.

Schoharie *Observer*, 1821-59.

Schoharie *Patriot*, 1840-69.

Schoharie *Republican*, 1843-44.

Severance, Frank H., ed., *The Holland Land Co. and the Canal Construction in Western New York*. Publications of the Buffalo Historical Society, vol. 14. Buffalo, N.Y.: Buffalo Historical Society, 1910.

Seward, Frederick, *W. E. Seward an Autobiography 1801-1846*. New York: Derby & Miller, 1891.

Seymour, Horatio, "Canal Report," *New York Documents, 1844*, VII, 177.

Shaw, Ronald, *Erie Water West*. Lexington, Ky: University of Kentucky Press, 1966.

Simms, J. R., *Frontiersmen of New York*. Albany, N.Y.: George C. Riggs, 1882.

Smith, James H., *History of Chenango and Madison Counties, New York*. Syracuse, N.Y.: D. Mason & Co., 1880.

Smith, Ray B., ed., *History of the State of New York, Political and Governmental*. Syracuse, N.Y.: Syracuse Press, 1922.

Stanton, Henry B., *Random Recollections.* New York: Harper & Brothers, 1887.

State of New York, *The Erie Canal Centennial Celebration, 1926.* Albany, N.Y.: J.B. Lyon Company, printers, 1928.

Sullivan, James, ed., *History of New York State.* New York: Lewis Historical Publishing Co., 1927.

Turner, Orsamus, *Pioneer History of the Holland Purchase of Western New York.* Buffalo, N.Y.: Thomas Jewett Co., 1849.

Van Buren, Martin, *Autobiography of Martin Van Buren.* New York: Chelsea House, 1983.

Van Buren, Martin, manuscripts. Library of Congress, Washington, D.C.

Van Wagenen, Jared Jr., *Golden Age of Homespun.* New York: Hill and Wang, 1963.

Waggoner, Madeline S., *The Long Haul West: The Great Canal Era, 1817-1850.* New York: G.P. Putnam's Sons, 1958.

Warner, George, H., *Military Records of Schoharie County Veterans of Four Wars,* Albany, N.Y.: Weed, Parsons and Co., Printers, 1891.

Weston, Richard, *A Journey West of Utica in the Mid-1830's.* 1833.

Whitford, Noble E., *History of the Canal System of the State of New York, Together with Brief Histories of the Canals of the United States and Canada.* Albany, N.Y.: Brandow Printing, 1906.

Woodcock, Thomas P. *Some Account of a Trip to the "Falls of Niagara" Performed in the Month of May 1836.* New York: private printing, 1840.

Wright, Benjamin, H., *Origin of the Erie Canal Services of Benjamin Wright.* Rome, N.Y.: Sanford and Carr, Printers, 1870.

Wyld, Lionel D. *Boaters and Broomsticks, Tales and Historical Lore of the Erie Canal.* Utica, N.Y.: North Country Books, Inc., 1986.

———, *Low Bridge! Folklore and the Erie Canal.* Syracuse, N.Y.: Syracuse University Press, 1962.

———, *The Erie Canal A Bibliography.* American Canal Society, 1978.

ಬ ಬ ಬ

Edward A. Hagan is the author of five other works on Schoharie County history and was editor of the *Schoharie County Historical Review* from 1981 to 2001.

An art teacher who wrote an unauthorized history of his ship at the end of World War II, he became a history columnist for the Middleburgh (N.Y.) *News*. He self-published *Pride of the Valley* (about Schoharie Valley railroads, in 1973); *War in Schohary 1777-1783* (the revolutionary war, 1980); *Hot Whiskey for Five* (civil war, 1985); *St. Catherine's Roman Catholic Church 30th Anniversary* (1991); and *An Alarm of Fire* (Middleburgh Fire Department 1995).

Edward died on May 19, 2002, his greatest historical challenge incomplete. For more than twenty years, he researched the

Edward A. Hagan

life of Governor William Bouck. A summary, outline, and typed notes and photocopies of source materials were found in five ring binders. Mark Sullivan completed the book and Lester E. Hendrix edited and arranged it for publication.

Sullivan has been a contributor to the *Schoharie County Historical Review* for fifteen years. A native of Central Bridge, N.Y., he is a Command Sergeant Major in the United States Army, Korea. He reviewed Mr. Hagan's materials, did additional research, and expanded Edward's summary into a book.

Hendrix retired in 1997 after thirty-two years as a journalist. He wrote the history of Schoharie County with his wife, Anne Whitbeck Hendrix, for the county historical society, in 1987. He succeeded Mr. Hagan as editor of the *Schoharie County Historical Review*.